little books for

BUSY MOMS

Juggling Tasks, Tots, & Time

Resources from MOPS

Books

Beyond Macaroni and Cheese
A Cure for the Growly Bugs and Other Tips for Moms
Getting Out of Your Kids' Faces and Into Their Hearts
Loving and Letting Go
Mom to Mom
Meditations for Mothers
A Mother's Footprints of Faith
Ready for Kindergarten
What Every Child Needs
What Every Mom Needs
When Husband and Wife Become Mom and Dad

Little Books for Busy Moms

Boredom Busters
Great Books to Read and Fun Things to Do with Them
If You Ever Needed Friends, It's Now
Kids' Stuff and What to Do with It
Planes, Trains, and Automobiles . . . with Kids!
Time Out for Mom . . . Ahhh Moments

Books with Drs. Henry Cloud and John Townsend

Raising Great Kids
Raising Great Kids for Parents of Preschoolers Workbook
Raising Great Kids for Parents of Teenagers Workbook
Raising Great Kids for Parents of School-Age Children Workbook

Gift Books

God's Words of Life from the Mom's Devotional Bible
Mommy, I Love You Just Because

Kids Books

Little Jesus, Little Me
My Busy, Busy Day
See the Country, See the City
Mommy, May I Hug the Fishes?
Mad Maddie Maxwell
Zachary's Zoo
Morning, Mr. Ted
Boxes, Boxes Everywhere
Snug as a Bug?

Bible

Mom's Devotional Bible

Audio

Raising Great Kids

Curriculum

Raising Great Kids for Parents of Preschoolers *Zondervan*Groupware™
(with Drs. Henry Cloud and John Townsend)

little books for

BUSY MOMS

Juggling Tasks, Tots, & Time

MOTHERS OF
M♥PS.
PRESCHOOLERS
...because mothering matters

MARY BETH LAGERBORG general editor

written by CATHY PENSHORN

ZONDERVAN™

GRAND RAPIDS, MICHIGAN 49530

We want to hear from you. Please send your comments about this
book to us in care of the address below. Thank you.

ZONDERVAN™

GRAND RAPIDS, MICHIGAN 49530

www.zondervan.com

Juggling Tasks, Tots, and Time
Copyright © 2001 by Cathy Penshorn

Requests for information should be addressed to:
Zondervan, *Grand Rapids, Michigan 49530*

Library of Congress Cataloging-in-Publication Data

Penshorn, Cathy, 1960-
    Juggling tasks, tots, and time / written by Cathy Penshorn; Mary
Beth Lagerborg, general editor.
        p. cm. — (Little books for busy moms)
    Includes bibliographical references.
    ISBN 0-310-24178-2
    1. Mothers.   2. Mothers—Time management.   3. Mother and
child.   I. Lagerborg, Mary Beth.   II. Title.   III. Series.
HQ759 .P463 2001
306.874'3—dc21   2001026808

Published in association with the literary agency of Alive Communications, Inc.,
7680 Goddard Street, Suite 200, Colorado Springs, CO 80920.

Interior design by Melissa Elenbaas

Printed in the United States of America

---

01 02 03 04 05 /❖ DC/ 10 9 8 7 6 5 4 3 2 1

To my mother,
Carolyn Seay Kopper,
who taught me that mothering is fun!

Contents

Help for Busy Moms

ONE OF MY FAVORITE segments on *Sesame Street* was a man who directed traffic during rush hour in a busy neighborhood of New York. With his white gloves, crisply ironed shirt, official hat, and broad smile, he brought harmony to the chaos with the fluid movements of a symphony conductor.

As cars drove past him, he'd call out "Good mornin'!" or " You have a GOOD day!" He greeted pedestrians at the crosswalks with a compliment, a smile, and a "Beautiful day, isn't it!" His joy was infectious, and he showed me what an impact a person can have when he or she approaches life's daily tasks with a sense of high calling and of serving others! Imagine how many crashes he averted—both emotionally and literally—while saving time for each person.

Moms are family traffic controllers. They ensure the traffic flows smoothly in the right direction. In cars, on bikes and scooters, in walkers, crawling, and on foot, family traffic comes at a mom with different needs and speeds, and from several directions, especially during morning and evening rush hours. And Mom knows that her attitude as well as her efficiency will keep the troops happily on track.

This little book by Cathy Penshorn helps busy moms like you find the crucial balance between the need to nurture your families and keep them moving forward, while fulfilling the other worthy commitments that zoom around you. Cathy's wise words also help remind you that mothering is a high and holy calling.

At MOPS International (Mothers of Preschoolers) we believe that better moms make a better world. To be the best they can be, moms solicit advice from parenting experts and mothers and grandmothers. But sometimes the best help of all comes from other moms who, traveling the same road, have made some great discoveries they're willing to pass along. Thus the series Little Books for Busy Moms was born. We've chosen topics to meet the needs of moms, presented in a format you can read quickly and easily. Like this one. To be a better mom, you need help juggling tasks, tots, and time. Enjoy! This book's for you, Mom.

Mary Beth Lagerborg
Publishing Manager,
MOPS International (Mothers
of Preschoolers)

Personally Speaking

"THERE'S TOO MUCH to do," I thought as I arrived home from the grocery store with three small boys and began unloading the car. Juggling the groceries and my wailing, hungry infant, I gave up on answering the ringing phone and marveled at the way everyone and everything seemed to need me all at the same time. As I sat down to feed the baby, I remembered the ice cream—melting in the July heat of the car!

Yes, I live in the same world you do ... a world of sticky fingers, toys scattered throughout the house, and a carload of "essentials" every time you leave home. We are in those nonstop days of motherhood when there's too much to do and not enough time or help to do it all the way we used to. We stress over untouched tasks as we watch the piles grow around us—the bills, the laundry, the unread newsletters and important papers, the toys, oh, the toys—and we wonder how to handle it all. We find ourselves late for appointments, losing patience with our children, losing hope for ourselves. We long for control over our days again, a chance to be with our husbands doing something fun, and the satisfaction of completing a project instead of just starting it.

Be hopeful! While your days of motherhood will never be as uncomplicated as your days before children, simple strategies can gain you back valuable time so that you can capture and celebrate the joys of motherhood amid the frustrations.

I am a mother, like you. And like you, I also juggle numerous other responsibilities and job descriptions. I keep the tax and bookkeeping records for my husband's dental office and handle all of the bookkeeping for our ranch. I keep us up-to-date with county and state regulations and order and pick up maintenance parts, supplies, vaccines, and feed for cattle, horses, cats, and dogs. Then there are the "on call" demands that require me to hastily rearrange our day so I can assist my husband: a young patient knocks out his teeth in a bike crash after dinner (I grab the diapers and the playpen as he says into the telephone, "We'll meet you at the office in ten minutes") or an animal gets sick or injured and needs immediate care (I take the baby to the neighbor and pull out the vet box; this is a two-person job).

Like many of you, my husband and I are involved in our community. We participate as volunteers at church and school functions, and our sons play on recreational athletic teams. We have responsibilities to our families of origin. Additionally, for four years I led a team of twenty young moms who served another one hundred young moms through MOPS (Mothers of Preschoolers) during nine months of the year.

The specific demands on your time are likely different from mine, but they are probably crying loudly for your attention, and like mine, sometimes seemingly in conflict with caring for small children. As a MOPS coordinator, I have talked frequently with young moms about their time management questions. I know that when I became a mom the standard answers regarding time management failed to help me with the dynamics of caring for babies and preschoolers, especially when I mixed children with the demands of my other responsibilities. Let's face it, it is impossible to carry on a business conversation with a crying infant in your arms! It's equally hard to write a proposal with toddler interruptions every five minutes ("Mommy, tie my shoe"; "Mommy, fix this"; "Mommy . . . !").

In those early years of mothering I watched every mother I knew and tried every idea I could think of in the hope of finding some approaches that might work to keep family life running smoothly. When I found something that worked for me, I was glad to pass on the discoveries I had made.

From that beginning came an outline of ideas on time management specifically geared toward mothers, especially young mothers with new babies and small toddlers. These little ones of ours are adorable but not at all helpful to us when we have to juggle our tasks with our tiredness. We need some new nontraditional ideas. Traditional approaches to time management teach the following principles:

- Delegate as many tasks as you can to someone else.
- Eliminate your interruptions.
- Handle every piece of paper only once.

These ideas work fine in the workplace, but I have news for them . . .

- Mothers have no one to delegate to.
- Mothers have walking, talking interruptions.
- Mothers don't have the option of handling ANYTHING only once!

We need different tools. We need ways to handle several priorities that are all "first." We need ways to plan and organize that don't put us in a box and make us feel guilty when all the "to do" stuff doesn't get done. We need ways to make our day accommodate our children's attention spans. Whether they are six months old, six years old, or sixteen years old, our children impact our day and we must figure out a way to work with them instead of against them, even as we train them for adulthood.

I pray that this book will *encourage* you as you face the demands of motherhood. You should find freedom in these pages—the freedom to be a creative, spontaneous woman and still move your family through the requirements of each week. Most of all, I hope you will find the freedom to *enjoy* your children more than ever as you juggle your tasks, tots, and time.

Acknowledgments

THE CHANCE TO ENCOURAGE moms on this topic seemed too good to be true when it was first presented to me. This book represents several years of listening to moms, observing, and speaking to MOPS groups around the San Antonio area. Each year I learned something new.

I would like to thank the following people for their support and encouragement:

My husband, Mark, and our sons Tommy, David, and Steven, who helped carry my load during the publishing process so I could meet deadlines. It is such a privilege to live with the four of you; you bring joy to my life!

The pastors, elder board, and members of the Women's Ministry Council at Northeast Bible Church who believe in the MOPS ministry and who guide and counsel me in my leadership there;

Geneva Albrecht, Paula Billingslea, and Jeanne Hogue, who served MOPS with me as Mentor Moms and whom I love dearly;

The MOPS steering team members with whom I served at Northeast Bible Church. Many of you now live all across the United States and overseas. I miss you even as I delight in the memories of the years we had figuring out together how to be moms!

Dianne Benac and Dawn Overman, who have hoped for several years that this book would happen someday; thank you for your many prayers;

My parents and sisters, Bruce and Carolyn Kopper, Betsy Duzan, Nancy Champion, and Susie Ecklund, and sister-in-law, Kay Vincent, who always cheer me on!

Elisa Morgan and Mary Beth Lagerborg at MOPS International, who have been faithful encouragers through the intense and unfamiliar publishing process;

Sandra Vander Zicht and Brian Phipps at Zondervan, who offered their professional insights to this project with care.

It is only by God's grace that this book was written, for it is he who led the way through this very challenging year.

CHAPTER 1

Juggling Priorities

THE AVERAGE AMERICAN MOM is well acquainted with the battle over priorities. Everything in her life screams, "Do me first, I'm more important than that other thing!" And if you desire to serve people or meet their needs, it's hard to walk away from a situation in which you know you can help. What's a mother to do when she can't do it all?

None of us can do it all. We are finite beings with a limited number of days. Our society would like us to think that it is possible to do it all, but it isn't; not all at once. We must choose to do some things now and other things later. Not doing it all means not doing it all *right now!*

So, how do we set priorities and then choose among activities, people, and responsibilities that are *all* important to us? It's not easy. You can start by thinking about priorities in two categories: the general priorities that are more far-reaching, and the daily priorities that directly impact this hour of this day.

GENERAL PRIORITIES

Sit down with your husband (or with a trusted friend, if you are single) and talk about the important parts of your life, those that are necessary and meaningful. It may be finishing a degree program, it may be time together, it may be recreation or family commitments.

Urgent versus Important

As you do this, separate the *urgent* from the *important*. Urgent refers to a task or demand that compels you to act upon it immediately. It is insistent. It is demanding. It may or may not be important. A telephone or alarm clock are good examples of the urgent; they insist upon an immediate response. Important refers to something of great value. It is significant to someone either now or later or both. It may or may not be urgent. Taking care of your marriage by spending time with your husband is important. It has long-term value, but it frequently doesn't seem urgent.

Distinguishing between the urgent and the important is necessary because the urgent is *always* more insistent than the important. If we are not careful, we will fill our lives with urgent activities that really don't matter in the long run. Decide what matters to you; look hard at what is important and recognize where the urgent is trying to distract you from it. This is an issue that increases in intensity as your children grow older, so if you can recognize and deal with it now, you will have an advantage later.

Involvement in Activities

Consider how many activities you wish to be involved in. Think about how each impacts your week, and what kind of preparation and travel time is involved.

Identify the pulls in your life that are currently *not* priorities. Many great opportunities for our families call to us. Identify the activities or requests that do not fit in your personal priority scheme at this time, in spite of the fact they are great programs. Then, when they come calling, it will be easier to turn them down without feeling guilty because you have objectively decided that for right now (this week or month or semester or year) they are not on your short list of important stuff.

Stress Factors

Identify the stress factors in your week. Do you have too many activities, too many work commitments, too many social engagements, not enough help? Is your schedule too unpredictable? See if you can nail down what it is that is stressing you out.

Conflicting Priorities

Look for potential conflicts between priorities that conflict with each other. For example, getting more sleep (maintaining your own health) may conflict with giving good care to your baby. Parenthood is full of hard choices and personal sacrifices in the best interests of your children. The early years are particularly demanding.

Where possible, alternate one priority over the other so that you can keep up with both. Take turns getting up in the night, or ask your husband to get up on the nights he's not going into work the next morning; take turns going to church Sundays when the children are sick so you both get the teaching there and have a turn with the benefits and challenges of a slow family morning with a sick child at home.

Sometimes the conflict is balancing caring for aging parents and caring for your own children. As much as you would like to, you can't physically push a wheelchair and a stroller at the same time without tipping one of them over! More and more young moms are facing this dilemma, and it has no easy answers. If you are in this situation, take a hard look at your schedule, at the demands of all the players, and at the sacrifice required by everyone—you, your spouse, your children, your siblings, and your parents. With all of the people involved, no one is going to be entirely satisfied. Work together on a weekly basis to find solutions.

Leaders emerge in families just as they do in other groups of people. If you are a leader in your family of origin and everyone looks to you to take charge, you will have to set some boundaries on the amount of work you can do. Once you are clear about the six tasks you cannot handle for Mom and Dad, the others are likely to step in—but they will wait for you to contact them. If you are overloaded with caregiving, it may be because you just took care of it like you usually do. Send up the red flag to your siblings if you are drowning. It's their responsibility to help too, but they may not know that you are ready for help. Likewise, if your parents are ill and your sibling is handling it all, offer to help instead of waiting to be asked.

Balancing Your Schedule

Look at this week's or this month's activities in the light of the above considerations and see what you can reduce or eliminate for now. It is okay to reduce the number of activities, commitments, and stress that you have each week for the immediate future. You aren't signing your life away; you are making some temporary changes in your schedule.

Where are you duplicating effort or overcommitting in one area? If family is important to you, continue to see grandparents, aunts, uncles, and cousins. But if family commitments are stressing you out, see them a fewer number of days each month. Or maybe it's stressful to see them all at once or to have a houseful of extra people. Take the baby to them for a visit, and then you can leave when the baby gets cranky.

Look for ways to spread out your time with friends. Meet a girlfriend for lunch with all the kids. Suggest that the men have lunch or breakfast together during their workweek. See a different couple on the weekend. Send notes or e-mails to keep up with friends you can't see that week.

Consider time for a hobby that can be balanced with the needs of your family. Whether it's fishing, antiquing, sewing, woodworking, golf, or biking, see if it's possible to help each other find time for that in your month. (More on this in Chapters 8 and 9.)

Balance your needs across a week or several weeks. Notice where different activities may meet the same need in your life. Select a *limited* number of activities that together meet different needs. Your child shouldn't need three weekly playgroups, even if she's an only child. You shouldn't need to see friends one-on-one every day. Your husband shouldn't need a baseball league and a basketball league and a golf league simultaneously. Have the courage to set, together with your husband, some boundaries on an average weekly schedule. Remember to save time and energy for the requirements of life: mowing the lawn, putting gas in the car, fixing meals, and changing diapers.

DAILY PRIORITIES

After we've established that finding time to clean the house is important, how do we actually get it done between 6 A.M. and midnight?

Ask yourself, *What is important right now?* It might be changing the baby or walking out the door to be on time for an appointment. Go do it. When you are finished with it, ask yourself again, *What is important right now?* Go do it. Soon the fog will clear.

Pick one goal each morning, and stick with it. It could be cleaning the kitchen, running a specific errand, or finding playtime with your oldest child. As you get your time management under control, you can pick a morning goal and an afternoon goal.

Keep a running list of other stuff that comes to mind as you are doing the most important thing. Write it down so you don't forget it, but don't detour away from your goal. (More on that in the next chapter.)

Do one thing at a time ... then do the next thing, then the next thing. Sometimes trying to do four things simultaneously clutters our brain. Focus on one thing at a time for now.

When you wonder which of your one hundred tasks to do next, do whatever increases your sense of contentment and order. If the piled-up dishes are driving you crazy, do them next. If you don't care about the dishes but you feel guilty or worried about the stack of bills on the dresser, deal with those next. Clear your head of the emotional overload and then you will be able to decide more easily about which of your ten priorities you should tackle after that.

Realize that your priorities *will* bump into each other on a daily basis. There's no way around it. When they do, you can pick the quickest one and get it out of the way or pick the one that takes the longest to finish and start making progress on it. Either is a good choice.

When you are called on to help with a project, always give yourself twenty-four hours to respond. Say, "I will call you back tomorrow with an answer." Few projects really need instant commitments, and you can balance this request against your other demands when you don't have the pressure of an instant answer. If you tend to avoid involvement outside your home, this gives you time to gather the courage to say yes. If you tend to overcommit to church or community activities, this gives you time to back away.

Practice saying out loud, "No, I can't help with that project right now. Thanks for asking, and please keep me in mind for next time." Think of the three huge benefits to saying no to some requests: first, you will be less crazy; second, you will enjoy the projects you agree to more; and third, women who don't normally get involved will step forward when others back away.

Ask yourself, *Does this activity or request fit with my life right now?* Will it fit better in four months? Will it fit better on a different day or a different time of day? Be assertive in juggling the elements of your day to fit with your priorities. For example, if naptime is a priority at your house, schedule everything else around it, without apology. A volunteer job that needs you at naptime is an easy decision; it doesn't fit with your priorities at this time.

Continually remind yourself what is important to you. The conflict between important and urgent will confront you on a daily basis. You will be comforting a child who smashed her finger in the door and the phone will ring. The child is important; the phone is only urgent. Let the answering machine get the phone. As you move through your day, ask yourself, *Is this task or activity or demand important or urgent?* Act accordingly.

Remind yourself that priorities are guidelines, not commandments. It's okay to violate your own rules occasionally, but if you do it often, you are not being honest with yourself about your priorities. Go back and reevaluate them again.

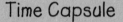

Time Capsule

Establishing priorities for our families can truly bring freedom to our weeks. It can give us a sense of purpose and direction and meaning to the sometimes dull and meaningless parts of our days. Within the framework of these priorities, we can then start to bring more order to the hours of our days and the days of our weeks.

CHAPTER 2

Planning with a Palette

ONE OF MY SISTERS is an artist. In preparing to paint, she gathers all the colors she thinks she might need onto her palette, a thin board on which an artist mixes paints. As her idea develops, she uses these colors alone and in many combinations. Sometimes she blends blue with red to deepen the purple in a shadow, sometimes she adds a dab of yellow to green to make grass appear sunlit. Sometimes there are colors on her palette *she never uses at all*.

Think of your week as a painting. To use your time well, you need to gather all the colors you think you might need onto one palette so you aren't chasing around after them when it's time to use them. As a mother you juggle so many people, needs, and commitments that you can't possibly remember them all. What you need in the midst of this unpredictability is a palette of tasks, phone calls, and errands from which you can choose activities that will benefit your family.

Yes, this palette is a list in disguise. It is *not* your report card! It *is* a center for an array of tools that you decide you need for your week. If it turns out that you don't need to use one of these "colors" (tasks, phone calls, or errands), or you decide that it's just not as important as the others, then you, as the artist, simply choose not to use it. That errand has no more cause to make you feel guilty for skipping it than marigold yellow has cause to shout "You forgot to use me!" when my sister paints.

You are free to look at your palette/list and say, "I choose not to do any of these things. We're going to the park instead." Have you forfeited the need for a palette? Certainly not. Those same reminders are valid the next day and can be tackled in the new context of that new day.

CREATING A PALETTE

Buy a 4x6-inch spiral notebook or 4x6-inch legal notepad. (Both can be found with the notebook paper at the grocery store.) This size fits easily in most purses, has enough pages for extra sheets for the kids to draw on when they're fidgety, and is *much* easier to find than a single piece of paper. Plus, they come in a variety of colors that can brighten your day!

March 1-6

Tasks:
pay bills
computer log
note to Tina
tax update
USDA info

Calls:
jeanne
eye doc
pharm.
insur.
Cindy
Nancy

Errands:
grocery—formula & photos
Sears—order p/u
cleaners p/u
trophy store—bball
Walmart—3 bdays
jewlery store—watch repair

Place this week's date at the top center: *March 1–6.*

Divide your paper into three areas. Mine has a "tasks" column flush left, a "phone calls" column flush right and an "errands" section across the lower page. Adjust this format to fit you and keep the notepad in an easily accessible place—the *same* place in your house all the time! It won't help you if you can't find it. (Mine stays in my kitchen by the phone when it's not in my purse.)

Writing ideas down in a central spot is key. It works much better than jotting a phone number on the back of the preschool newsletter and compiling the grocery list on the service call receipt . . . neither of which you will find when you need it.

When you think of a call to make or an errand that needs running, write it down. Don't try to figure out *when* you are going to do it, because you probably don't know when; just get it written down.

Keep your palette handy when you are feeding the baby. Many times in this relaxed setting your mind will clear enough to remember other things you wanted to do, and you can write them down while you're sitting still. Sometimes feeding time brings with it the panic of all the things you are leaving undone! Either way, with your palette beside you, you can jot down those things and have peace that they will be accomplished instead of forgotten.

Limit your palette to a single page. If a group of ideas overtakes it and needs more room, then put "work on birthday party" on your palette and make a separate birthday party list on the next page that won't interfere with the other priorities of your week. Do this with the grocery list too.

ERRANDS

Your palette will also help you figure out how to get your errands accomplished without doubling your time in the car. Consulting your notepad, you can use the extra ten minutes you didn't plan on having after the dental appointment to run a nearby errand.

Group your errands to the same side of town. Accomplish several stops in one area.

Stop and think about the places you shop. We all get in a rut and continue to shop in the same old places without realizing that there may be a similar store more convenient to our current traffic pattern. I shop at one grocery store during the summer because it's close to our neighborhood pool but use a different store during the school year because it's closer to the school.

Consider each errand you run and ask yourself if there is a location at which you could accomplish two goals with one stop. You can get diapers and the birthday present at Wal-Mart if a birthday present is the priority today. If groceries are the priority, check the toy aisle at the grocery store for that birthday present.

Try a major errand day once a week instead of lots of little errands all through the week. I discovered when my firstborn was about a year old that we were wearing ourselves out running errands many days each week. Part of the problem was that we live on the outskirts of town, and any trip took us twenty minutes just to get to our first stop. The shortest errand I could run would still take between forty-five and sixty minutes. I decided to try a marathon day to see if it worked better. I packed a morning snack for my son, scheduled a fun stop for lunch at either a playground or park, and saved the "quieter" errands for after lunch so he could sleep in his stroller while we finished up. This pattern continued to work for our family, so even when I was packing and unpacking *three* boys, we still did marathon errand days. Over ten years we have had errand days that didn't go well, but overall the concept has worked well for our family.

However, every mom has her own tolerance level for errands and long days, and every child has an opinion about going with her! If a marathon day doesn't work for you, find a pattern to your errands that does. If you have an early bird child, do your errands all before lunch and then have a peaceful afternoon at home. If your child doesn't think clearly until after lunch, make a play date at the park after lunch, or even after naps, and then run errands until Dad gets home. Consider your family's strengths and preferences, and then do what works for you.

Pack an easy sack lunch on errand day so you can celebrate your progress at the park or playground and save money at the same time. If everyone wears out before you get to the park, and you decide to quit and go home for naps, you can picnic in the front yard. The kids will enjoy it anywhere!

Always allow more time than necessary for *everything!* Build a buffer zone into your arrival and departure times. It takes six times as long to do anything when accompanied by small children, so just figure that into the equation. My rule is to plan what I think I can do, then eliminate at least one thing.

CALENDARS

Use a simple, one-block-per-day calendar that allows you to see at least one entire week at a glance.

Keep only *one* calendar. I don't care how big it is, whether it's in your purse or in your home, but keep only one. If you keep two, you invariably write different activities down in different places and don't find the conflicts until it's too late to avoid them. Some moms prefer the newer electronic calendars. Use something that suits you and is easy to change, because it will change often!

Note the morning commitments at the top of each day's block, the midday or after-school commitments in the middle, and the evening commitments at the bottom. This allows you to see at a glance that you have four evenings committed already this week and that means you are *full!* It also keeps you from missing the important morning meeting at the preschool that you noted at the bottom of the square and didn't see until 10:30 A.M., by which time you had missed the meeting.

Write in "stay home" on some days of your calendar, especially if you feel trapped in the "too busy" syndrome. That reminder on your calendar will help you keep the priority you established for yourself and will help you remember that your stay-home time is as valuable as your away-from-home time.

PHONE CALLS

Group your short phone calls. Make all five of them one after the other and get them over with.

Make your short calls in the morning so that the person you are trying to reach has all day to call you back. You are more likely to finish this piece of business today that way.

Check your errand list, and see if you can save yourself time by making a phone call instead.

When your children are very small, be present in the room with them when you are on the phone. You will be able to hand them toys while you talk, and they like both your physical presence and the sound of your voice. As they get older, say age three, the phone becomes a competitor to them. Save phone calls that will require lengthy conversation for times when the kids are busy with an activity of their own.

Similarly, limit the number of calls you make from the car when your kids are with you. Instead, use that time to talk or listen to music with them. When you talk on the phone in front of your children, you tell them they are not as important to you as the person on the phone.

PLANNING THE WEEK

Planning is one of those ironic words for mothers. It's humorous to consider planning, because life seems to have a plan of its own, but look at your plan as a starting point, knowing that it is likely to change. Without a starting point, you don't have a good handle on which direction to turn next.

Think across the span of the week instead of pinpointing lots of activities for individual days. Plan a few highlights for one or two days, like MOPS on Monday and seeing the pediatrician on Wednesday. Be spontaneous with the rest. I usually sit down on Sunday nights to redo my palette for the week. Sometimes I notice a conflict waiting to happen or recognize how I can merge our errand running with our fun things to minimize our time in the car. Flexibility is key. Some weeks, the errands that on Monday seemed most important never happen because the situation changed. Sometimes phone calls become unnecessary. You never quite know what the week will bring.

Plan only the first half of your day and be "spontaneous" with your palette during the second half of your day. I sometimes leave for playgroup in the morning not knowing for sure if we will come home for lunch and naps or catch lunch out before we run errands. It depends on everyone's attitude and energy level. Similarly, I plan the clean-out-the-closet project for the morning, knowing that there may not be energy left in the afternoon.

Find a point of no return for the day when you stop doing new things and finish up all the odds and ends you started earlier in the day. When my children were little, that point was about 4:00 P.M. At that point everyone was up from their naps and we would finish folding those last few pieces of laundry, finish building the tower we started after lunch, finish making the cookies, and finish watering the plants. Notice the key word here . . . *finish!* If we had started a new project at this point in our day, the ones already under way would not have gotten finished.

Finally, remember that *you* are in charge of your day; your children are not. One of the most helpful mothering tips my mother ever gave me was this: "You are the mother; their day can revolve around what works well for you." While we don't set our children up for frustration, neither do we need to accommodate their childish perspective on what is important every hour of the day. You are the mother. Let your child's day revolve around the priorities you and your husband have set.

Time Capsule

My friends and I joke that when we make plans we know we're only making "Plan A" and that whatever we decide will change several times before the event actually happens. This is the nature of planning for mothers. But we need to have a plan, a course of action with which to start, or we will be tossed about by either the whims of our children or the influences around us. Find a place to start. Make a plan. Adjust it as necessary. Develop a palette that works for you—one you can keep up with and that you will use. Give yourself room for the unexpected as you plan your week. Be sure that enjoying your children is part of the plan.

CHAPTER 3

Thinking in Pieces

"WAAAA, WAAA, WAAAA.... *(long* silence, deep breath) *WAAAA, WAAAA!*"

"Okay, okay, there's a baby here somewhere who wants to be picked up," I thought as I struggled to wake up and deal with the sound of crying. It was my three-week-old nephew, Jared, and his mom had him well taken care of by the time I finally woke up. But living with him for just seven days brought vivid memories of newborn days rushing back to me.

My youngest was only two years old, yet I had somehow already managed to forget the nonstop demands of a newborn. They are hungry every two hours; three, if you're lucky. They need new diapers at least that often. When they are not asleep or eating or being changed, they want to be carried around to be sure you won't leave them. And they are oblivious to the needs of their siblings and parents, the requirements of the household, and Mom's "discomfort" following delivery!

We learn quickly with a newborn that the minutes we can devote to our other tasks and responsibilities are few and far between. The difficulty of starting and finishing a task persists through the early childhood years and is a source of frustration to many mothers. To cope with this reality, start thinking of tasks in pieces. Like a jigsaw puzzle with a hundred pieces, our days become a series of child-size increments that, put together, eventually create a picture. But it is a slow process with *lots* of pieces. Let's look at these pieces of family life first and then see how newborns specifically fit into the puzzle.

SEE THE PIECES

Almost any task has several steps to it. As mothers we must take those steps one at a time, instead of waiting to accomplish the entire task at once. For example, a good friend of mine who had two preschool boys wanted to make curtains but was overwhelmed by the size of the project. As we talked, we broke the project into very small pieces:

- look for a pattern (she had done that) and consider fabric;
- buy the pattern and consider fabric;
- look at more fabric;
- choose and buy the fabric.

These small pieces fit into her week.

Once she had purchased her pattern and fabric, we again broke the project down into time segments small enough to fit into naptime and other short moments of her day:

- lay out first section and pin;
- cut first section;
- lay out second section and pin;
- cut second section;.
- sew first two sections.

Once she caught the vision of how she could make progress over the weeks with small pieces of time, she was encouraged and actually flew through the project. The curtains look great too!

This idea translates into practical applications throughout our home:

- When cleaning out the car, do the trash piece one day, vacuum or spray down the mats another day. Restock car essentials like Kleenex and hand wipes on grocery day.

- Tackle mending projects one at a time instead of letting the pile grow into a mountain. You can sew on a button or award patch in ten minutes while the children play in the sandbox.

- Divide preschool, church, and volunteer projects into several steps. Read the instructions one day. Gather the materials another day. Review the lesson and project a third day before presenting and teaching it.

- Plan birthday parties two or three weeks in advance. Think through each piece of the party time: the people you would like to invite; the games, if any, you would like the kids to play; the food you will serve; the decorations you would like. Write down the supplies you need and shop for them over the three weeks. A little advance thinking will allow you to prepare for the party in pieces and enjoy it more when it arrives.

- Expose your children to new skills in short sessions. Riding a tricycle or throwing or kicking a ball can be a five- to ten-minute adventure. Sometimes we feel guilty that we "don't have time" for a particular activity. But we do have *short* pieces of time—and we can make good use of them if we narrow our expectations and attempt a smaller piece of the bigger activity.

We must break down every single thing we do into small five- or ten-minute steps because five- or ten-minute intervals describes the reality of our day. This is enough time to move a task forward and leads to the first of five important mothering mottos covered in this book: Progress counts!

PROGRESS COUNTS!

It takes more effort to accomplish routine tasks than it did before you had children. You have child-ish, unhelpful help and many more distractions, not to mention a toddler's tendency to spill juice on a freshly mopped floor. Remind yourself that *progress counts!* The floor may be sticky under the table again, but it is less sticky overall than it was an hour ago. It's important to see the pieces of progress and value them almost as much as completion.

On a day-to-day basis, think of your tasks in pieces, and ask these four questions:

What piece of today can I do with the kids *around?*
What piece of today can the kids do *with me?*
What piece of today do I need to do *alone?*
What can be working for me while I'm doing something else?

For example,

You can make phone calls or exercise with the kids *around*.

They can *help you* set the table or make jello for dinner.

You may have to balance the checkbook *alone*. (I do!)

Your oven can be baking the dinner while you play outside with the kids.

Once you have asked these questions, you can choose what you are going to do next.

What Can I Do with the Kids Around or Helping Me?

Most of our day happens with the kids around or helping us. There is value in our children helping us even though it is simpler and quicker to do it ourselves. Sometimes we can proceed alone with our projects while they are around and playing, and sometimes we should find ways for them to help.

Laundry

Make a game out of the laundry. As you sort the clothes, let the kids put each piece into the washing machine. Yes, it might take a little longer, but part of the value in mothering is in shared experiences. Doing laundry together for ten minutes instead of five is not a waste of time.

Buy a dozen plastic baseballs to keep in the laundry area of your house. Whenever you do the laundry, let your children play laundry ball—throwing the balls into a laundry basket on the floor. This is great fun for toddlers and will allow you to sort and fold in peace. When you are finished, you can play too!

Another fun use for the laundry basket is to pretend it is something else. Your child can pretend it's a car and take a stuffed animal for a ride or pretend that he's racing fast around the corners (and sometimes turn so sharply that he tips it over!). It could be a princess carriage. Have your child sit in it and act out the Cinderella story as you tell it. Or how about turning it upside down as a zoo cage with stuffed animals? This game could follow you around the house as needed!

When the laundry is dry, take it to a central place in the house to sort. Send the children to get their dump trucks, strollers, and wagons. As you sort (but don't carefully fold) the laundry, let each child deliver a few pieces to the appropriate room: Dad's socks to his room, brother's shorts to his bed, and so on. Be aware that few clothes will stay neatly folded from the time you sort them out to the time they reach their destination, so don't have them deliver clothes you are really picky about. This approach will complete one more piece of your laundry project and you can have a good time doing it together. When you visit each room later in the day you can fold the clothes and tuck them into dresser drawers. As your children grow older, they can learn this step too.

If you visit a laundromat, use that time as game time, book time, or coloring time. Without the distractions of other household demands or the phone, you can focus completely on playtime with your children while waiting for the laundry.

Make your ironing part of a play date with another mom. Who says we have to iron alone? It makes much more sense, especially with very small children who are in danger around an ironing board, to have two adults in the room anyway. You can take turns ironing, supervise the kids together, visit, and return home with freshly pressed shirts and a sense of having accomplished one extra thing today. *That* is good juggling!

Mealtime

Even though we've all prepared meals while balancing a child on one hip, most of us would agree that we would prefer not to. Cooking is so much easier using two hands! How can we juggle mealtime better with small children around?

Find a getting-ready-for-dinner activity that frees you from hands-on effort with your children. Play dough and coloring books work well for this time, as the children can be within view but not in need of your help. Keep these activity supplies handy to your kitchen.

Invest time in teaching your children how to help in the kitchen; it will save you time sooner than you think. Even a two-year-old can learn how to find the cookie sheet and roll up the Pillsbury crescent rolls. When he's three, you may find this can become "his job," and it's one less thing you have to prepare for dinner. Look for the short, simple jobs that don't involve sharp utensils.

When you have your children help you in the kitchen, use oversize bowls. These will contain the splashes created by small helpers and minimize the mess that naturally occurs when little ones are learning to cook.

Let your three-year-old learn how to set the table. It won't be perfect, but it will be close enough and will give her a sense of contributing. In *What Every Child Needs*, Elisa Morgan and Carol Kuykendall write, "Work is family stuff. When you assign responsibilities even to small children, you communicate that they are valued and needed in order for the family to continue on."[1]

I would never have tried this with a child as young as three except that I had no choice. During my third pregnancy, I was placed on bed rest the week before Christmas. For the next ten weeks I lay in bed and on the couch. I couldn't stand at the sink and pour myself a glass of water without provoking labor pains. For our family to function, every little task counted, and our two sons, ages five and three, pitched in to help their dad. Both learned quickly how to set the table, along with a number of other tasks, and we made it through with a *lot* of help from our friends.

Have a "kids kitchen" in your kitchen so your kids can play along while you do the real thing. We have a drawer full of kitchen toys and a small table nearby that they use as a countertop, restaurant window, lunch table, or cooktop.

Use baby swings, door gates, and playpens to keep children in sight but not in your arms while you're cooking. A high chair is a great place for a baby to play while you cook dinner. Pull his high chair close to where you are working, so he feels like he's part of the action but isn't close enough to grab pots or be splattered by hot grease. Even if he is small, he can roll toys across his tray and generally "supervise." I give more suggestions on this topic in Chapter 6, "Teaching Children to Play Alone."

Finally, as you seek ways to minimize your time in the kitchen, fix enough for two meals when you cook. Do this often, whether you're fixing pancakes, spaghetti, tacos, or salad. It doesn't cost any more money each week to fix enough food to feed your family the same meal twice, but it saves you half the time! Serve one today and put one in the refrigerator for two days later. Even families that don't like leftovers can handle it if you give them a day or two break between the first meal and the second serving. You'll gain back valuable time in your week without any additional planning.

Interruptions

Interruptions are a way of life for parents, especially during the years of small children. That said, thinking in pieces helps reduce interruptions because you are actively working with smaller increments of time. You are accommodating the probability that you will have to stop soon and are in essence interrupting yourself before your child does, which will actually lessen your frustration with her and with your task. What other tricks might we add to this portion of our juggling routine?

Address your children's physical needs before you start a task. The baby doesn't purposely get hungry or fill his diaper as you start something else. Take thirty seconds to assess her physical needs before you dive into the next thing.

As they get older, prepare your children for the times when you are unavailable. Tell them, "I have to talk to Daddy on the phone for a few minutes. Is there anything you need before I call him?" You have met their needs first; they can wait until you are available again.

Teach your children when and how they may get your attention, both during a task and during a conversation. Give guidelines and patiently enforce them. It will take a while for kids to change the interrupting behavior! Teach them how you want them to approach you when you are

>talking with another adult;
>talking with a different child;
>talking on the phone;
>busy with a task; or
>doing a task that is potentially dangerous to them.

In the kitchen, for example, they need to learn not to come hang on your arm or purposely startle you when you are using a sharp knife.

Give them a *simple* polite entry to use (such as "Excuse me" or laying a hand on your arm) and respond quickly when they use it. Look them in the eye and say "Just a minute" or return the physical gesture, putting your arm around them or your hand on theirs, and expect them to wait. During this training time your initial response will be most effective if it is immediate.

Give them a buzzword to use when someone is hurt or there is a true urgency to their need for you. Consider "Problem!" "Come Quick!" "Mayday!" or some other phrase that has meaning to your family. Again, expect this to take a while for children to learn.

As children get older, enforce consequences for repeated interruptions outside of the guidelines you have set. I sent my boys to sit in chairs when they interrupted my phone conversation the third time. They had to stay in the chairs until my conversation ended and I came to get them. There were days they sat there a *long* time! Eventually they stopped interrupting my phone conversations.

Know that interruptions are a way of life for mothers. We can reduce them, but we will never eliminate them.

What Piece of Today Do I Need to Do Alone?

There are pieces of every mother's day that are preferable to do without the supervision of our little ones. As you consider the pieces of your day, think ahead to when you need those moments alone so you can plan them to fit with the tasks you need to accomplish that day.

For example, I do some of the bookkeeping for my husband's business while I am at home. It is not my strength, so I have to gear up for it. If I save it for the late afternoon when my energy is low, I'll never get it done. So on days when I know I must bring the tax information up-to-date on the computer, I will arrange our day so that I have alone time in the morning to tackle that project.

Look at parts of meal preparation and other household projects that require your attention alone and do them early in the day. This way, you can get everyone involved in the rest of the project later on. We use this theory on the weekends as my husband and I spend time in the morning bringing various jobs to a point where our sons can help finish them up in the afternoon.

What Can Be Working for Me While I Do Something Else?

The dishwasher, the sprinklers, the washing machine, the bread maker, the oven ... all these machines can work for you while you tackle something else. The key is to start them *first!* Put the chicken in the oven before you take your afternoon walk. Start the sprinklers before you start lunch.

This will delay the start of your next task. The baby may have to cry in her crib for three minutes while you finish loading the washing machine, or your three-year-old may have to set up Candyland by herself while you load and start the dishwasher. However, your time together will then be uninterrupted and your machines will be working for you while you play.

Finally, look at the timing of things that run themselves. I used to run the dishwasher at night and then unload it in the morning. But when my first-born started preschool, I found I didn't want one more thing to do on those mornings we were trying to get out the door on time. So I started running the dishwasher after lunch. This allows me to have little hands help with the unloading part while we're fixing dinner and, for me, works much better. Experiment to see what timing patterns work best for you. It has to work for your family, not someone else's.

ADDING A NEWBORN

My husband says that with the birth of each child, every family has to find a "new normal." Whether it's your first baby or your sixth, when that little one arrives, a new dynamic has entered your family, and *everyone* has to shift a little. The reality is that you now have the same number of hours in the day to divide between more people. This means they have to share you more. The thinking-in-pieces concept works especially well with newborns because their needs are so continuous. In addition, take to heart these time management tips during those first few months with the baby.

Focus on the bare necessities of life, whatever they are for you. Pare down your week to the basic tasks for a short time as you get to know this new little one and figure out how to direct your family in its new setting.

Find a way to take time away from the baby for just a little while each day. Let Dad hold him after dinner while you soak in the tub or take a brisk walk around the block. Even twenty minutes will help your outlook.

Create a means for the baby to follow you around without being carried all the time. I loved holding my babies and I carried them a lot. I chose to do lots of tasks with one arm. But other times my arm was *tired*, and it was time for them to watch without being held.

For those times, I used their cradle (which rolled into any room in the house), a bouncy seat, the car seat carrier, or a baby swing. From these vantage points they could sit and observe all that I was doing. They were safe, fed, had a clean diaper, and knew I was there with them. Sometimes they got bored watching and went to sleep; sometimes they protested *loudly* that they wanted to be held. Frequently they received a long explanation from me about why they weren't getting picked back up just yet.

Were there times that I gave in and picked them up and changed my activity in frustration? Absolutely. We *all* have those days and weeks. But over time, infants learn that Mom has responsibilities that require them just to be there and be patient.

Be aware of the intensity of your sleep deprivation. Look for ways to refuel yourself. Whenever possible, sleep when the baby sleeps. My own mom's theory is that "Naps are for mothers!" You will be more effective if you sleep when the baby sleeps and then move him around the house with you as you do your tasks, phone calls, and errands. It is good for him to learn that he is a vital part of your world but not the center of your universe every moment he is awake.

Keep the noise level of your household at its usual volume. Babies can sleep through most background noises, including pots and pans rattling, vacuums, and televisions. If you make the house completely quiet when he sleeps, you'll set him up to sleep only when it's totally quiet, and that is *not* realistic. Let him learn right away to sleep amid the chaos of a family, and you will be able to use your time when he's asleep more effectively.

Accept help when it is offered. Babies are a reason for rejoicing and a great motivator for people to help each other.

Be highly selective in the few special activities you choose to continue with your older children as you acclimate the baby to her new world. Ironically, something that you used to do every week with the older one may actually become more special when you back off and do it once a month.

If your baby hits a colicky stage, call in the reinforcements! Ask a neighbor, relative, or friend to come to your house and either take a round of walking around and around the house with the crying infant or help you deal with all the tasks that are undone and driving you crazy while you walk with the baby. One or two hours of extra adult hands in your home can make a huge difference in your outlook. Depending on your situation, you might request your husband's help catching up during a couple of hours of his nonworkday.

Know that, for the moment, your week has been sliced into tiny, tiny tidbits of time that will lengthen as the baby grows. As much as you can, enjoy this stage while it is here; it will never come again.

Time Capsule

Because we mothers have demands that are equal in priority, we can't always finish one task before we start the next. Therefore, we have to think of everything in small steps, stages, or pieces. While tasks take longer to finish than before, we are actually accomplishing more during the course of a week by doing small pieces of lots of different jobs. Only you know the limit to how many different pieces you can juggle at once without dropping them. Work within your limit for now. As you become successful with those, you can add more.

CHAPTER 4

Taming
the Clutter Monster

I WALKED THROUGH MY "clean" house today and counted the items on the floor: three small wooden train engines, two trees for standing alongside the railroad track, a few Duplo blocks, five books, one plastic monkey, and two crayons under the kitchen table; that was the downstairs. Does your house look like mine? Is there life beyond the drop-it-and-run stage of preschoolers?

Clutter becomes a time management issue for moms because we lose so much of our time to cleaning up and cleaning up again. For those who are highly organized and neat, the sheer volume of odds and ends you step over can be a source of stress and frustration that keeps you from enjoying this stage of parenting. For those who organize by piling and prefer the freedom of less structure in your home, the additional number of piles that children bring can send you over the edge of despair after a while. Regardless of your natural bent toward neatness and organization, children will magnify the issue tenfold.

The good news is that there are a number of simple steps we as mothers can take to return a sense of order to our home and therefore reclaim some of the hours in our day lost to searching for misplaced items. Let's start with the obvious.

TOYS, TOYS EVERYWHERE

Have a reachable "home" for every toy, crayon, car, and teapot. Make toys *easy* to put away. If the children can't put it away, you will have to do it. Experiment with different kinds of containers and shelving systems for different kinds of toys to see what works for you and your family.

At our house . . .

- plastic storage bins with lids hold train pieces, farm sets, and army guys;
- open shelves store board games already boxed and large self-contained toys or series of toys, like all the Batman vehicles;

- a lidless box that you can keep stuffing things into contains costumes;
- a medium-sized trash can in the closet holds weapons (toy bows and arrows, Davy Crockett guns, light sabers, etc.) that store best standing up;
- one drawer in the kitchen stores all the kids' kitchen supplies; and
- another drawer in the kitchen holds crayons and coloring books.

At our house, shelves don't work for costumes, and plastic storage bins don't work for crayons and paper. Find what works for you.

Baskets work well for collections of stuff: baby toys, matchbox cars, books by the rocking chair, beanie babies. They are easily accessible and easy to put away.

There are lots of storage possibilities for Legos and Duplos, all available at your nearest discount store:

- Large plastic storage bins with lids.
- Plastic silverware dividers. These allow you to sort blocks by color if you want to. You can also stack the trays in a larger plastic bin with a lid.
- A three-tiered toy bin on casters. This can move from room to room, and the bins are fairly shallow and easy to dig through.

- A large plastic drawer unit, my current favorite for Legos. The unit stays put in your child's room or toy room, but the drawers themselves can be carried anywhere in the house and are easy to dig through for that certain Duplo truck driver or blue four-button piece.
- Duplo buckets. Save these for traveling. They are so deep that they have to be entirely dumped out to find the pieces; however, they have strong carry handles and their narrow shape makes them compact when you are packing the car. They are great for taking to Grandma's house or on a road trip, but not the best for daily use around the house.

If your children have *lots* of toys, consider putting some toys away for a while and limiting their choices. Then periodically switch the toys. Not only will they be less overwhelmed with the clean-up time, but they will enjoy playtime more as they can focus on fewer possibilities.

Accomplish this same purpose by simply moving toys to a new room every once in a while. It's amazing how a new environment can sometimes change a child's perspective on an old toy.

Clean up as you go, rather than leaving it all until lunchtime or dinnertime. It's much less overwhelming for the adult and the kids to pick up one game at a time instead of six.

Involve children in the cleanup as young as you can. My son Steven was too little to tackle a clean-up project on his own at one and a half years, but he could still help.

The "pile-it" stage, when two- and three-year-olds love to pull everything out of a closet and dump the contents into one giant pile of toys, drove me crazy. It was really hard for me to allow this, but I did because I observed it to be universal among so many different children. I did, however, require that my sons pick up the pile *before* they moved on to other things. If they were still happily playing and pulling from the pile, fine. But if they abandoned the pile to head outdoors, I called a halt to the outdoor adventure until the pieces of the pile were returned to their homes. This balance worked for us because it allowed the kids the freedom to act their age but didn't dump the enormous load of cleanup onto my shoulders at the end of the day.

Have a small table or shelf for the kids' "in progress" games and projects. Anything they want to work on over time can go there, one project per child. This idea becomes more necessary as your children grow older and build Lego creations, because they will not want to break apart the masterpiece they just finished.

When you are faced with a major pick-up effort, choose an upbeat song, tape, or CD to play as the family clean-up song. We surf our way through the house to the Beach Boys!

Have an "odds and ends" bucket, basket, or box for yourself that you can toss things into over the course of the day. (Things like the items I picked up off the floor this morning.) Have one child play delivery person with those items at the end of the day, returning them to their appropriate spots. This could be a good job for a younger child while an older one sets the table for dinner, or they could trade those jobs each evening.

If you live in a two-story house, have an upstairs bucket or basket that sits on the bottom step. Fill it with these same odds and ends that go upstairs, then have someone deliver the items back to the rooms at dinnertime.

Embrace this season of chaos with photos. Take some photos of your "toys everywhere" days so you and your children can look back and laugh, and so they can see the freedom you gave them as toddlers. I especially love the ones depicting an entire room taken over by an expansive train set with a village built of blocks next to the stuffed animal zoo near the Batman and army camp—photos that show my children's developing imaginations, creativity, and building skills.

Finally, adjust your expectations of your home a little bit through this stage. As long as I have children at home, there will be stuff to pick up, step over, and clean. During this season, when the children are just learning how to help with it all, I have learned to be patient with them and myself. For many more excellent ideas on taming the clutter monster, pick up the book *Kids' Stuff and What to Do with It* by Leigh Rollar Mintz in this Little Books for Busy Moms series.[2]

MOM'S DESK AS MISSION CONTROL

When the space shuttle astronauts leave the earth, they trust Mission Control in Houston, Texas, to be their central point of information and communication. We all need a mission control.

Look around your home and find an area—probably somewhere in your kitchen—that you can consider your own Mission Control Center. This needs to be *your spot and no one else's*. This is where you keep your calendar, frequently called phone numbers, some way to handle the mail, scrap paper, and your palette/list. Having a focal point for all these planning and information pieces will gain you back more time than you think because you won't be searching the house for them.

The major discount stores and office supply retailers all carry a variety of divider trays for papers. I prefer using the vertical dividers that stand papers up instead of the horizontal trays that lay papers down flat because when you fill a stack of trays with papers, it's very hard to see the ones under the top tray. When you use a side-by-side divider, you can see each slot fully.

These work great for mail and any other notices you need to keep track of. I use one section of the divider for regular bills, one for bank statements, one for correspondence, three (one for each boy) for school notices, soccer schedules, and permission slips, and one for miscellaneous papers. That way when I walk in the door with the mail, I can stand at my desk and, without even opening the mail, sort that day's arrivals into the correct slot or the trash can. Now there's one less pile on my desk, and when my husband, Mark, wants to know where the utility bill is, I know exactly where to find it.

The main benefit to using a divider stand or tray is that it will get full of stuff and you will have to clean it out! A pile on the desk can always get bigger, but a tray gets full. When you are forced to sort through it before you are "behind," it is less over-whelming, which takes us back to dealing with life in manageable pieces.

FINDING A SENSE OF ORDER

Regardless of where you are living, you probably find peacefulness in one or two places in your home.

Mentally walk in the front door of your home and ask yourself, *What gives me a sense of order here?* Is it neatness in the front hall? A swept floor? Sofa pillows in place? What gives you a sense of order in your own home? Two things matter to me: I need my bed made and the kitchen counter clean. If those two places are in order, I can handle almost anything else out of place. Make keeping order in those significant places a priority. It will change your outlook on everything else.

Ask your husband which places matter to him. What is important to his sense of order and makes home a refuge to him when he comes home at night? The answer may surprise you. I used to spend lots of time helping the kids pick up toys off the floor in the family room before Daddy came home but didn't focus at all on the kitchen. When I finally asked Mark what would help him relax at the end of the day, he amazed me by saying it was the condition of the kitchen floor. He cared more that the kitchen floor was swept free of the day's light dusting of dirt and crumbs than that the toys were out of the family room. What do you know? This had not been my priority, but I made it become priority over the toys in the other room since it was important to him.

SPOT CLEANING

Finding time to clean the whole house with lots of little helpers around is hard. The littler they are, the harder this seems. It helps to think of your housecleaning in very small increments. If you spot clean one room at a time, you can actually clean the whole house over the span of a week without having to tackle much of it at once.

Keep cleaning supplies in each bathroom and on each level of your home. If you buy one or two cleaning supplies each grocery run, eventually you will have enough to spread out around the house. While it may crunch your cash flow at first to buy more supplies, you will save noticeable time by not running back and forth between the cleaning supplies and the rooms to be cleaned.

When your child is old enough to sit in the tub and play without being held, you can clean the mirror and sinks and toilet while still watching him in the tub. While he rolls around in his towel after his bath, you can spray down the wet tub, give it a scrub, and be done. *Voila!* . . . one clean bathroom. (Be sure to secure supplies behind childproof locks or in high medicine cabinets.)

Invest in tools that work and that you will actually use. If you don't mop because your mop doesn't work, get a different one. If you don't sweep the kitchen because your broom brings in dirt streaks from sweeping the front porch, get another broom so you have one for the porch and one for the kitchen. It's only silly to have two if one is never used. If they serve different purposes, and therefore are both used to the betterment of your sanity, then the extra eight dollars is worth it!

Similarly, find cleaning supplies that work well for your various household surfaces. Different spots need different chemicals to lessen the amount of work it takes on our part to get things clean. A spray with a degreaser works well in the kitchen, but doesn't make the bathroom job any quicker. I can spend half the time on my sons' tub if I use a textured cleaner like Softscrub instead of an all-purpose spray, because the spray takes forever to cut through the dirt that collects there.

Keep dusting supplies on each level of the house so you can nab those spiderwebs that you notice on the curtains when opening the shade after your child's nap. A little bit here and there goes a long way.

Keep cleaning rags in each bathroom. They will be handy for all kinds of messes and save you digging them out from a central spot on short notice.

If you have a two-story house, have a diaper-changing spot on each floor. Equip them both with diapers, wipes, diaper pail, and so on. Change diapers only in those two places. This not only assures that you have all necessities at hand, but it also gives your child a consistent expectation of how to behave during diapering time. If you try to diaper on the floor in the living room, it's hard for a little one not to squirm toward her toys. Take her to the diapering place, get it done, and send her back to play.

Vacuum early in the day, even right before lunch. If we don't get it over with early, we won't do it. Vacuuming is hard on our backs, it's loud, and it's disruptive. Pick a day of the week to be vacuum day, tackle it by itself, and be done with it. You'll feel ahead of the rest of the cleaning once it's done. If you have a two-story house, do the downstairs one day and the upstairs another day, unless you get on a roll. Do the stairs when you do the level with the least carpet.

Several moms have asked me about vacuuming around babies. Babies actually handle the vacuum better when they are asleep; it just becomes one more background noise. So try vacuuming about the time they are ready to wake up and see what happens. Don't stress about vacuuming when they are awake, either. Just be reassuring to them if they are afraid and let them watch from a distance.

GETTING OUT OF THE HOUSE

So you've fed everyone breakfast, got them dressed, and now it's time to go. Ten minutes later you find yourself finally backing out of the garage wondering why you are late again! What takes so long when we try to get out of the house?

Know that you are not alone. Across the country thousands of other mothers are pulling out of their garages ten minutes later than they had planned. Part of it is the size of our children (they take twice as many steps as we do, their arms hold half as much), part of it is their slower pace, and a big part of it is how little they can do for themselves. It is not a matter of simply picking up your purse, walking out the door, and stepping into the vehicle. More likely, you have to carry or lead each child and whatever supplies they need until you return, correctly buckle them into the car, double-check that you have your keys, the baby's bottle and formula, and that the house is secure, and *then* you can leave. Whew! No wonder we're tired by the time we hit the street!

This process won't change until the children are bigger, but here are some ideas to shorten the process of leaving.

Pull together the necessities of the day *long* before it's time to leave. If you're leaving first thing in the morning, pack up the night before; if you're leaving after lunch, pack up before lunch.

Have your fussy dresser pick out her clothes the night before. Include in this selection your daughter's hair ribbons and other accessories so there isn't an argument the next morning.

Have your dawdling preschooler dress himself *before* he plays or watches television or videos. If he refuses to do this, calmly take him by the hand with his clothes to a room away from the toys and tell him he may return to the toys when he is dressed. Then walk away. Try this for the first time on a day when you don't need to be anywhere at a specific time, because he may pitch a fit or try to return to the toys in his pajamas. Remember, your goal is to stay calm. Your child has the choice to get dressed and play, or to *not* get dressed and *not* play. Either way, you are both leaving the house at ten o'clock. When he figures out that he gets more playtime by getting dressed instead of sitting in the laundry room, he'll do it.

Plan on at least five minutes for the actual leaving process. If you need fifteen minutes on the road to be on time, plan to start leaving twenty-five minutes before your appointment: five minutes to load up and leave, fifteen minutes to drive, five minutes to unload and arrive with children at the next door! If you start leaving at 10 A.M., you will arrive at 10:25 A.M., not 10:15 A.M., because it takes those extra five minutes on either end to manage the kids into the equation.

Keep a designated container by the "exit door" (whichever door gets you to your car) for odds and ends that need to go with you next time—a fresh travel pack of tissues, the cleaner's receipt, audio-tapes that belong in the car, a dish to return to a friend, and so on. A basket hung from the doorknob works well, or you could use a bucket, box, or portion of a shelf.

Get a rack with enough hooks for all the children's coats and bags. Hang it by the back door, low enough that each child can reach his or her own hook. Their stuff will be ready and easy to find.

Have a "basics" bag in your car—two diapers or pair of underwear, some wipes, two toys, and a cup or bottle of water. This will lighten your load when you want to make a quick dash to the grocery and save you the time of having to pack a full diaper bag. Refill the basics bag when you get home so it's ready to use next time.

Do one *less* thing before you leave. I struggle with this more than anything else in my time management. I always want to do one *more* thing. Doing one *less* thing gets me out the door on time.

Slow down your adult pace to better accommodate their childish pace. Your children are not seeking to frustrate you; the pace at which they function is simply slower than yours. Unfortunately, you are the only half of the equation that can understand that, so take a deep breath and know that someday they will be waiting on you!

Time Capsule

As long as we have children, we will have messes to step over and clean up. As mothers, we have to balance tolerance for our children's child-likeness with training for their future; then we need to add enough order for the adults in our household to function effectively. If you can add some order, one place and situation at a time, to your home, your days will run more smoothly for everyone.

CHAPTER 5

Playtime Is Valuable Time

I Took His Hand and Followed . . .

My dishes went unwashed today,
I didn't make the bed,
I took his hand and followed
Where his eager footsteps led.
Oh yes, we went adventuring,
My little son and I,
Exploring all the great outdoors
Beneath the summer sky.
We waded in a crystal stream,

We wandered through a wood,
My kitchen wasn't swept today,
But life was sweet and good.
We found a cool sun-dappled glade
And now my small son knows
How Mother Bunny hides her nest
Where fern and larkspur grow.
We watched a robin feed her young,
We climbed a sunlit hill,
Saw cloud-sheep scamper through the sky;
We plucked a daffodil.
That my house was neglected,
That I didn't sweep the stair,
In twenty years no one on earth
Will know or even care.
But that I've helped a little boy
To noble manhood grow,
In twenty years the whole wide world
May look and see and know.

—ANONYMOUS

This poem speaks volumes to me. When we start looking at time management as a concept, it's easy to assume that every minute must be tangibly productive. However, when it comes to mothering, that's not true. Good time management includes time spent playing with our children.

PLAY EVERY DAY

Not only does playing with your children build trust and relationship, it also teaches them to balance work and recreation. No matter how much work there is to do, it's important to abide by mothering motto number two: *Play every day.*

Get down on the floor while they are learning to crawl, and crawl with them. Play peek-a-boo behind the couch so they can crawl over and find you.

Spend time in the sandbox. Take off your shoes and let your kids bury your legs in the sand. Build a mountain out of wet sand and try to dig a tunnel under it. Create roads for matchbox cars. (Warning: Once a matchbox car has been in the sandbox it will never be the same; you might consider designating nonfavorite cars as sandbox cars.) Build a model of your neighborhood in the sandbox.

Have a squirt gun fight in the backyard. Be sure *you* get wet.

Turn on some upbeat music and dance in the kitchen. Jump around in circles until you are dizzy.

Read to them.

Make play dough together:

1/2 cup water
2 cups flour
1 cup salt
1 T. vegetable oil

Knead the above ingredients well and add the desired food coloring. Store in a sealed container in the refrigerator; it should last indefinitely. (It also comes out of the carpet and clothes better than the store-bought kind.)

Play follow the leader, hopping around the house.

Forget the gourmet dinner you planned; make cupcakes with them instead.

Pull on old clothes and old tennis shoes and go outside and stand in the rain; splash in the puddles with them.

Build forts with sheets (they work better than blankets because they are lighter-weight). Use clothes-pins or safety pins to pin them together, over folding chairs, and around doorknobs. Crawl under the fort and read a book by flashlight. Enjoy a picnic lunch of apples and fish crackers (they vacuum up well!).

Take a walk in your neighborhood or around a nearby park.

View life from a child's perspective. Mud, for example, is interesting stuff. It looks funny, feels funny, smells funny. It's like play dough. Mud on good clothes does not make moms happy, and neither does mud on the carpet—but mud outside can be fun.

Rejoice in the little discoveries of each day, like sugar comes out of the bag really *fast* when it's full and not so fast when it's not full. Cleaning up spilled sugar works better when you sweep most of it up with a broom and then wipe the rest with a towel instead of dumping water on it first.

Work on gross motor skills. Spend time helping them learn how to throw balls, peddle a tricycle, or do aerobics or dance steps. A toddler can learn the five basic positions of ballet. Practice with her.

Fine motor skills are important too. You can "finger paint" with shaving cream on the kitchen table.

Tape butcher paper, wax side down, onto the kitchen floor. Use watercolors and fat brushes for a great beginning painting experience.

Use butcher paper taped to the floor to create life-size drawings of your kids. Have them lie down on the butcher paper while you trace around them. Expect lots of giggles. When you have finished tracing, fill in a few details and let them color themselves. Then they can hang their portrait on their bedroom door. It won't be a masterpiece, but it will be fun!

Read to them again.

ONE-ON-ONE TIME

Author and child psychiatrist Dr. Ross Campbell teaches that children need one-on-one time with their parents; he calls it focused attention.[3] I have found this to be true. But how do we find time for just one amid the demands of many?

Capitalize on the times when only one child is awake—first thing in the morning, when a younger one is napping, or after an older one wakes up from naptime. Study the pattern of your household and see where you can find opportunities for time with just one.

Read books in bed with the first one awake if you are not rushing off to school first thing in the morning.

Trade child care with a friend, or schedule a time with your husband, so you can take just *one* child to the grocery store. Stop for a doughnut first. Twenty-five cents and a game of tic-tac-toe or a conversation will help that child feel like she has had you all to herself for a long time.

Do puzzles before naptime with the older child after the younger ones are in bed.

Focus on that particular child's interests: coloring, throwing balls, riding bikes, playing with dolls, or animals. Do what he or she likes to do for a while and ask questions about it:

- What do I do next?
- Tell me about this piece or person. What is his job?
- Does this animal like to play tag or dress-up?
- What kind of a birthday party would this toy have?
- Which animals or people are friends? What do they like to do together?

Recognize that you will be bored with some of the things your child likes to do, but hang in there. Your child loves it when you are willing to be in his world.

GET THEM STARTED, KEEP THEM GOING

Part of teaching your children to play alone (which is the subject of the next chapter) is playing *with* them first, to show them the possibilities in their world. Then, when it is time for them to play alone, they can repeat the activities they have learned with you.

Show them how to use their imaginations with toys and costumes. Reenact story lines from books you've read together or movies you've seen. Even simple baby books have a story you can retell to them: "This little duck went out to play . . ." using a stuffed duck.

Using their toys and stuffed animals, reenact adventures from life such as going to the zoo or to a birthday party or to the park: "Now the family is driving down the highway to the park. Now they get there, which gate should they go in? . . . What are the girls going to play on first? . . . Okay, let's make these two blocks the seesaw . . . here they go . . ." Ask questions and let the children respond.

Once your children have caught on to this idea, leave them for a little while to play the next part by themselves: "Now you take the kids to the sandbox to build a castle while I check on dinner, and then I'll come back and see what's happening." Be sure you come back. Investing time like this will pay you hours of dividends in time you can use while your kids are happy playing on their own.

Demonstrate a toy to children younger than toddlers, then let them have a turn. Little ones love noise!

Actively build their attention spans. Few children are innately gifted with a long attention span. It is more their nature to move from one stimulus to the next. But an attention span can be developed without crushing a child's quest for discovery by showing them how to find a new use for the current toy. Sit down with them when they are frustrated with a toy and help them solve the problem. Point out a new way to build a block tower. If they are tired of towers, build a garage or a castle or a dollhouse.

Show them new possibilities with the toy they are playing with. Try to extend this activity just a few more minutes so they catch the vision that there are always other possibilities.

Protect Your Fun Time

Protect your playtime with your children. It communicates to them that they are important to you and that they have intrinsic value relative to the rest of the world. If you had a business appointment with an adult, you would not expect to be interrupted by other adults. Similarly, we must respect our time with our children.

That said, some playtimes are going to have interruptions. But if you can make them the exception rather than the rule, you *all* will be less frustrated and you will feel more in control of your time.

Choose a period of time with your child that you can really be committed to. Ten minutes may not seem like much, but it counts.

Decide before you start playing whether or not you will answer the phone. Your child will feel very important if you choose to not answer the phone during your Hi Ho Cherry-O game.

Prepare your children for interruptions you know are coming: "We can start our game, but I know Grandma is going to call soon, and I have to stop and talk to her when she calls," or "After we get this side of the fort built I have to stop and move the front yard sprinklers while you start the second side." This will help reassure them that they are your priority even when you have to step away for a few minutes.

Start your machine tasks first so they don't interrupt you midproject.

Stay focused on the priority of the moment, giving your attention to this specific child and her game/project of choice.

TIME WITH DAD

A father can strongly shape a child's view of herself or himself. Some dads are intimidated by the baby stage of parenting and, depending on their own background, are not sure how to interact with their small children. Others are very comfortable from the start but still like fresh ideas for time together. Encourage your husband and children to discover and deepen the camaraderie you know they can have, even early on.

Set aside some family time for Dad to spend one-on-one with each child. One is less overwhelming than two or three or four.

Point out to Dad how each particular child can "help" him, or suggest an activity Dad would enjoy (or tolerate!). Maybe the baby is learning to crawl, and the two of them can play hide-and-seek around the family room couch. Maybe your one-year-old is learning to roll a ball back and forth. Maybe the two-year-old can hold the hose and sponge and help wash the car. Maybe the three-year-old can sit on Dad's lap and they can play on the computer together.

Teach your child about the special place Dad has in your family. Make Dad's homecomings after work and his days off a *big deal!* One family I know has a race to the door every day when Dad arrives to see who, Mom included, can hug him first. It brings a smile to his face even when he talks about it.

Prepare your child to do things with Dad. Teach her how to work a puzzle or build a block tower to "do with Daddy tonight."

Reinforce to your husband how much his children need him and love him and how glad you are that he is their dad. Be affirming of his fathering at every opportunity.

Have Dad read to them. Send them to the library or bookstore together so he can pick out a story he wants to read, maybe one of his childhood favorites or one that involves something he is interested in.

Ask Dad to help with the bedtime routine. His presence will make a difference to you and to the children. Ease him into it by asking him to read the bedtime story on alternate nights, do the toothbrushing, or hold the baby for twenty minutes while you help the older ones.

Leave the kids with Dad for a few hours periodically. Ask him if he wants ideas for how to fill the time and make suggestions if he requests them. Eventually he'll plan the time himself because he will know his children well.

TIME WITH OTHER ADULTS

When other adults invest time in our children's lives, they give a precious gift. Grandparents are the most obvious examples, but your family may have aunts, uncles, family friends, neighbors, even older cousins whose influence you would value for your kids. Find time for these people who can help you direct your children toward choices that will benefit them and protect them from harm. It's a long-term investment that will pay important dividends later. When your teenager is tempted by drug use, it may be the faithful uncle who played basketball with him once a month since he was three years old who is able to steer him away from the drugs, or the grandpa that he doesn't want to disappoint that makes the difference. Nurture these relationships now so they have credibility later.

Look for times to include these special people in your children's lives. Have them for dinner, invite them to your children's special events, create a play-time after naps when your child is likely to be happy.

Prepare your children for the time with these special people. Communicate your respect for them. Reassure your child that they are lovable and trustworthy.

Give grandparents and other adults a realistic picture of what to expect from their time with your children: "We're in a building stage where all he wants to do is play with blocks" or "She loves to be read to" or "Why don't you two find a bucket and shovel to take to the playground so you can scoop rocks while you're there."

Remind yourself that adults who don't live with children probably don't remember all the child-rearing details that you know. So if it's important to you and your child, *say it!* Remind them that a six-month-old can't have honey or that your one-year-old is not yet safe on the stairs.

Start with shorter visits of perhaps an hour, and let them grow as everyone becomes more comfortable with each other.

Provide for everyone's physical needs. If the baby is hungry, he is not likely to respond well to Aunt Lillian when she arrives. And she won't be patient with him if her arthritis is acute or she doesn't have a comfortable place to sit. Be aware of physical needs and try to meet them before they hinder the relationships you are trying to build.

Time Capsule

One of the balancing acts of motherhood is finding quality time with our children amid all the responsibilities of running a home. Recognize that time spent just enjoying your children for who they are today is a valuable use of your time. In five years you won't remember how often you cleaned the house, but you will remember the adventures and daily activities you shared with your child. Remember our mothering motto—play every day!

CHAPTER 6

Teaching Children to Play Alone

PART OF YOUR TIME management strategy should be teaching your children the benefits of being alone. It is not your job to be a full-time entertainment director for your children. Not only does being alone foster great imagination, but it has the potential to become a shield in a world of pressure to conform and participate in activities that destroy. As a mom, you know how good it is to have time by yourself—you are probably begging for some time alone right now. Give your child the tools to be content alone also.

FILL THEIR TANKS FIRST

Dr. Ross Campbell teaches that children have an emotional tank that influences their behavior. When that tank is full, the child *feels* more loved and is therefore more secure and able to function in healthier ways within his world. Campbell proposes three elements necessary to fill these emotional tanks: eye contact, appropriate touch, and focused attention.[4] I have found when I do these things first, my children are more content and more likely to function well without my attention.

The first element, eye contact, is so important. How often do we say to our children when they are misbehaving, "Look at my eyes"? We want their full attention. We need to give them that same attention when we are praising them and loving them. Let your children see your eyes and smile when you say, "I'm proud of you," "You did that well," or, "Thank you for helping me." Listen to your children with your eyes as often as possible. They will *feel* your love more deeply when you do.

The second element is appropriate physical contact and touching. As babies, our children are held all the time. As they grow, we carry them less, but they still need physical closeness. We need to find new ways to touch them. It doesn't have to be a hug; we can tousle their hair, give them high fives, pat them on the back or leg, or put an arm across their shoulders. All of these give them the reassurance that we still love them as much as ever. One of the ways I do this is by sitting very close to my kids when we do puzzles, play games, or read books. I go for elbow-to-elbow contact in the midst of the daily activities of life.

The third element in Campbell's approach is focused attention: finding one-on-one time with each child. This is the hardest; however, it also reaps the greatest dividends. It's not unrealistic to spend fifteen minutes with each of three children during one hour and expect the others to play together without bugging you. They can be taught to understand, "This is Mommy's special time with Tommy. You've already had your turn." Start your one-on-one time with the youngest, because he will find it hardest to wait.

INITIATE TIME ALONE

The ideas in the previous chapter are foundational to helping your child fill her time alone. Often you need to start her on a project or idea, leave her for a while, then check in and play a while. In the meantime, you are getting your tasks accomplished in bits and pieces.

Set up their expectations for a given time frame. Give them a sense of order to their day, such as, "We're going to work on projects at home until lunch and then run errands and play outside in the yard."

Leave books accessible in stacks or baskets where your child can discover them. Small children will not seek out a book, but if they toddle into the den and find their books stacked on the coffee table, they might climb up on the couch with one and look through the pages on their own. Have a few of your child's books somewhere in every room of your home, not just on bookshelves.

Start when they are very young to give them playtime alone with you nearby but not interacting with them. Infants can

- sit in swings and look at mobiles,
- lie in their cribs and play with their feet while listening to music, or
- sit in a bouncy seat and bat at the spinners on the frame.

Babies can use this time to safely discover their world, while at the same time learning that Mom will not leave them when they are silent. Sometimes babies cry just to see if we're still around. If we can simply answer them in a reassuring voice, they will often settle down.

Use playpens, door gates, saucers, swings, jump-ups that hang from door frames, and other tools to keep babies nearby without being in your lap all day.

A high chair can be a great place for a baby to view his world. He doesn't have to sit there only when he's eating. Playtime in the high chair also works as a great introduction to dinnertime. It frees your hands for cooking, keeps him safe and nearby, and starts the process of his learning to entertain himself. A side benefit is that it builds the concept of waiting for dinner, which can be useful when you want to venture into restaurants. There will be days when he doesn't *want* to play in his high chair, but that's just life when you are a baby!

When they are about six months old and starting to sit up, establish a "fun place" for babies where they can safely explore toys on their own. We used a playpen filled with toys. It went to whatever room I needed to be in. The baby could play in it and experiment with his stuff, but if I needed to use the bathroom or step into the kitchen out of view, I knew he was safe. As he grew, the toys changed and the time in the fun place changed. This worked wonderfully during meal preparation because I could see him, he could see me, we could talk to each other, but I didn't have to hold him while I cooked. Eventually he could pull himself up and start to walk around the perimeter holding on. Each of the three boys *really* liked that discovery.

One friend used this as a structured part of her day with twins. At 10:30 every morning each baby would be placed in his own playpen with toys. The mom used the next hour to deal with the house and her other responsibilities without carrying babies! This went on for years and worked well for their family.

I know of other children for whom a door gate in the doorway of their bedroom worked to utilize their room as a fun place. Every child is different in the amount of stimulation needed and the length of time it will take to get them used to this idea. It's easiest if you begin doing it before they walk, but you can introduce the concept of a fun place at any time.

Be Committed

Every time I teach this idea I'm asked, "How do you get your kids to play alone and nap?" The best answer I have is that while I recognize that some kids find time alone harder to tolerate than others, I am deeply committed to the idea that their ability to spend time playing alone is in their best interest and, in fact, necessary to their well-being. Therefore, it doesn't bug me when they resist.

My children do *not like* getting vaccines at the pediatrician's office, even if they get a doughnut afterward! When they are two years old they do *not like* holding my hand in the parking lot or when crossing a street. I make them have the vaccines and hold my hand because I know both are good for them, whether they understand that or not. Their cries or temper tantrums don't dissuade me, even though I don't like that behavior. After a few times they realize they can't win this battle and they stop crying in the parking lot. If they know you are committed, they'll quit fighting, although some *will* prolong the fight longer than others before they give in.

Let me especially encourage you to try some of these ideas if you have just one child. It's so easy to work your day around her when there's just the two of you, but it would be better for her if you set her up to play on her own a while.

I saw this clearly in my own home with our youngest son during the years he was the only pre-schooler at home. The older boys, in contrast, always had a sibling at home during their preschool years. The daily dynamics were very different with one instead of two or three, and it was easy for me to accommodate his desires without a second thought.

One day I realized that he was becoming self-centered due to all my well-meaning but overdone attention. I had to back off and allow him more time by himself. (I also started taking my turn going first and letting him lose when we played games. It was a shock to his system to have Mom win, but it paid off as he learned how to tolerate losing.)

TEACH THEM TO PLAY TOGETHER

As your children grow, teach them to play together. This takes patience and time now, but it will pay off later. This requires sitting with them and walking them through the ways you want them to act toward each other.

Show the big one how to teach the little one. Maybe you are building a block tower together. Show the big one how to hand blocks to the little one and help him stack it. Or make a game of big brother builds the tower for little brother to knock down. Put big brother's masterpiece creation somewhere the little one can't get to it; like in his room or behind a door gate that the little one can't get in. (Another great use for playpens is as a safe harbor for older preschoolers to play where the younger one can't reach them!) Sit down with them together and teach them both how you want them to work together.

Look for activities that can involve both. Can the baby hold the clean plastic spoon and bang it on the high chair while big sister works with the play dough? A "holding job" is often enough to help the little one feel involved.

Show them how to work together and use their imaginations: One can be Batman and the other, Robin; one can be a circus trainer and the other, an animal to train (gently, of course!); one can be a cashier at the restaurant and the other, a customer.

Think ahead for Christmas and birthdays about toys that would work well for your children to play with *together*. One Christmas we gave our oldest son a Lego pirate ship (very complicated with lots of pieces), our middle son a Playmobil pirate ship (complicated but less fragile), and our youngest son a Fisher-Price pirate ship (very sturdy with fewer pieces). For months we had pirate wars at our house with each boy equipped to participate with his own ship.

REFEREE DISPUTES

When your youngest child turns three, you can teach your children the art of working through arguments. This requires coaching. Take them to a spot away from the point of contention (it can be out of the room, to the kitchen table, or any other convenient place away from the play place). Each child gets a turn to say what he or she wants from the confrontation ("I want the red truck now"). When they can agree on a solution, they can return to the play place.

Initially, you will have to help your children find solutions. Frequently the solution is taking turns.

My favorite is "You can have it first, if I get a longer turn later." The older one quickly realizes the benefit of going second, and all parties involved eventually learn that going first isn't always best. The beauty of this process is that children learn to work through their conflicts sooner to avoid leaving the play space. At some point they will choose to compromise on the spot so that they don't have to go to the kitchen table to work it out.

Use a kitchen timer to help establish sharing time. Sometimes it's just too hard for a small child to voluntarily let go of a toy. A five-minute turn that ends when the timer chimes is often the easiest on everyone and still gives the experience of trading back and forth.

Teach kids to respect each other, each other's toys, and each other's ideas. One child should not be allowed to destroy what the other has drawn, built, or dreamed up.

Similarly, older siblings have a knack for entering a game the younger ones have going and subsequently wreaking havoc with it. If the older one wants to join in, he can't change the rules or the game. He must respect what the others have started or come back later when they are ready to do something different.

One friend of mine told her small children to "respect the wishes" of a sibling when having a conflict. This idea appealed to me because it focused on "respecting," not "obeying," a sibling. If younger brother wanted to roll the dice himself, older brother was asked to "respect his wishes" and not be overly helpful. Likewise, if older brother had plans, the younger one was expected to respect those.

Allow each child to have some special items they don't have to share with siblings. Most things need to be shared; they belong to the family. But a few pieces should be set aside as only theirs. We put this limit on our sons' cuddle blankets. The others were not allowed to use, hide, or claim another's blanket. It gave each child a sense of ownership and drew a line in the sand that the others had to respect.

Give yourself permission to duplicate a few toys that are high-use, high-demand, one-child items. Two red fire trucks are a great investment in teamwork and will instantly eliminate the fight over one. Only you can decide if there is greater benefit to your family in having two or learning to share the one.

As your children leave the preschool years, allow them some time with friends of their own age without the younger ones tagging along or without having to supervise the younger ones. This can be occasional or frequent, depending on your family's needs. I am close to all three of my sisters, and I firmly believe that part of that closeness stems from my parents' willingness to give us our own space with our own friends when we were children. We sometimes shared our playtime and sometimes had a friend just to ourselves. A balance is most beneficial.

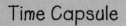

Time Capsule

Our children benefit when they can be content playing alone and when they understand how to interact positively with other children. Teaching them these things is our job. Fill their emotional tanks *first*, then lead them through the experiences of playing alone, sharing, taking turns, and resolving their conflicts.

CHAPTER 7

Naptimes and Bedtimes

FEW MOTHERS WOULD ARGUE the point that children need naps and early bedtimes. Their eyes, bodies, and behavior show their need for this extra sleep. Still, many children protest, turning naptimes and bedtimes into battlegrounds. How can we avoid this battle?

For starters, make a child's bed a haven of comfort and rest. Bed should be a *good* place to go, not a punishment. A child's crib or bed should hold his or her favorite blanket and animal, both of which should be off-limits as discipline tools. Your children will catch your attitude toward their bed immediately. If you say, "Your bed is so comfortable, I wish this were my bed!" they will value it. If you present their bed as a place to go when they are naughty, they will resent it. With this outlook, let's look specifically at strategies to make naptimes and bedtimes proceed more smoothly.

NAPTIME

Be committed. Know that it is in your child's best interest to nap. That's all the reason you need.

Be laid-back. An easygoing approach that communicates an understanding of their reluctance will get you farther than a rigid approach that expects them to *like* taking a nap every day. Instead of being a brick wall, be a brick wall covered in velvet—soft but unmoving. Use empathy as you say, "I know, sometimes I don't feel like a nap either, but we're going to take one anyway."

Be predictable. Most children work best with structure. Schedule a regular naptime if possible.

Work *with* your child's body's natural rhythm. A nap sometime shortly after they have eaten takes advantage of the body's tendency to slow down other functions while it digests food.

Instead of abruptly cutting them off in the middle of a game, give your child a five-minute warning that it will soon be time to pick up the toys and take a nap.

Telling them, "You have time for one more game (or book or play dough animal) before we take a nap" will minimize the trauma of stopping as they have time to bring their activity to a logical stopping point. This same transition time is important at bedtime too.

Read to your children before naptime. This accomplishes several things:

- it gives them the gift of being read to;
- it settles their bodies down, slows their heart rate, and prepares them to sleep;
- it provides a positive emotional transition to sleep;
- it gives them one-on-one time with you;
- it starts their exposure to books, which sets them up to become stronger readers when they start school.

Put the youngest child to bed first since he's likely to sleep the longest. Try reading separately to each child or alternating reading to them together and separately. See which works best. When my boys were two and a half years and six months, I read one book to them together at naptime because I couldn't stay awake through a second book!

If your child strongly opposes naptime, lie down with him for five minutes on the bed if he is out of a crib. This is time well spent, as it reassures him of your presence and keeps him in his space. Many children will settle down this way, but others will become inconsolable when you leave in five minutes. Try it for a week; if it still doesn't work, change tactics.

Tell your children, "I won't do anything fun until *after* naptime." This reassures them that they are not missing out because they have to take a nap.

If your children share a bedroom, find a way to split them up during this time. Put a playpen in your room or let one nap on your bed or the couch.

Use music or stories on tape to help them go to sleep. Again, this works for some reluctant nappers, while others will find this more stimulating than soothing.

As they grow older, allow children to take a limited number (one or two) of toys or books to bed at naptime. This way they can play quietly as they are settling down, and they will frequently play themselves to sleep.

Transition to "rest time" as children get to be three or older. Allow them to have more toys and books in their bed with them as needed. Tell them they can just "rest their eyes" instead of sleeping. Many will fall asleep; others will benefit from lying still and being alone. I still remember the day my middle son proved this point. We had been on the go until midday, and he was *grumpy!* Finally, I took him upstairs, way past naptime. He never slept; he just talked to his stuffed animals. After nearly an hour, he was a new child. He just needed some time alone.

As they move from two to four years old, adjust the starting time of your child's regularly scheduled naptime to accommodate their changing energy patterns. Your two-and-a-half-year-old may no longer be tired right after lunch but will run out of steam an hour later. Move naptime forward or backward as needed, overlapping naptimes for several children in order to give you some individual time with each, as well as some time alone when they are all napping.

Check the temperature of their room. It's hard to sleep if you are too hot! Cool it down, if possible, during this time.

Be aware of your children's activity level before naptime. Some kids come in from the park exhausted, fall into bed, and go to sleep immediately. Others have to cool down, slow down, cool down, slow down before they can crash. If you have a "headlong into life" child, observe how long it takes her to change gears, and adjust her schedule of activities accordingly. She may need more transition time before she can be still enough to fall asleep. Build that transition time into your day so she can actually *sleep* during naptime. Otherwise she will only *slow down* during naptime and then be grumpy for the rest of the day!

Use the car as needed for naps. If you are forced to pick up other children in the middle of naptime, and your child will sleep in the car, try leaving the house earlier than necessary. This may allow your child to actually sleep longer, even though he is sleeping in the car. If you leave early, take bills to pay, a book to read, or letters to write. If you have a cell phone, you can even return phone calls while you sit in the parking lot. You can get your stuff done, allow him to nap, and be to your pickup on time!

If your child won't sleep in the car, explore possible adjustments in your pick-up times for your older child or carpool with another mom in the same boat. If no solutions are found, you may have to just remind yourself that your baby will not be permanently scarred because his nap was cut short this one school year.

BEDTIMES

In her book *Raising the Curtain on Raising Children*, Florence Littauer talks in detail about the sacredness of the bedtime routine, referring to it as "the children's hour," as reflected in that poem by Henry Wadsworth Longfellow.[5] This is the last hurrah of the day. Everyone is wiped out, yet it is a great opportunity to teach loyalty and forgiveness and to give your children faith, hope, and love.

Make bedtime a positive time. Even when your children are very young, you can say to them, "Let's go find your nice, cozy bed and your warm blanket and you can have a good sleep."

Establish a routine for bedtime. When your children are tiny, you will probably feed them, perhaps rock them for a few moments, then put them down. As they get older, you might sing to them before you put them in their beds. (One of my sisters says, "Be sure to pick a song your baby-sitter will know!") The next addition might be to insert a storytime before bedtime.

As they leave the toddler years and start to dress and undress themselves, bedtime has the potential to take forever, because preschoolers are *slow!* At least when they were babies, you could keep the momentum going as you carried them around. Now that they are two, the whole process slows to a crawl!

Try a picture chart with a few simple tasks: toys, bath, and teeth. You can use foil stars from the grocery store to reward completion of each. Be sure *they* get to add the stars to the chart. (My dentist husband adds that you can allow your toddler to start chewing on his toothbrush and "brushing" his teeth *with water only* as soon as he has teeth. This will allow him to get used to the feel of the toothbrush in his mouth, and he is more likely to allow you to finish brushing them after he has had a turn. Do *not* use toothpaste until age three, and even then use only a small, pea-sized dab.)

Set a timer for the amount of time you think your child needs in the tub, and when it goes off, have him get out of the tub. As children get to be three and four years old they can "race" the timer. If they finish before the timer, allow them to pick an extra story to read or another reward suitable for bedtime.

Sometimes you have to add a negative consequence to the reward system. One idea for children who are four years old or older is to withdraw the source of their distraction as they get ready for bed. If your daughter gets sidetracked by the dollhouse and won't get her pajamas on, then she can't play with the dollhouse for twenty-four hours. Be sure to alert children ahead of time to any such ground rules.

My boys love races. They love racing *me* the most. The fastest way to get them to bed is for us all to start in the kitchen, and then race to see who can get into their pajamas and brush their teeth first. I find that sometimes I am more able to enjoy their story and nighttime routine if I have made the jump to pajamas too, even if I still have dinner dishes ahead of me.

Avoid making bedtime the time to clean up the whole house. Set aside other times throughout the day to keep ahead of the overall toy mess so that it is less overwhelming at bedtime. The bedtime routine should involve cleanup of their room only.

Be realistic in your expectations of bedtime tasks. Give children enough time to be unhurried. They don't need thirty minutes, but neither will they be happy rushing to do it in five minutes. We chose to compromise when it came time to pick up toys at bedtime. If the bedroom was a disaster, we agreed on piles, or selective cleanup. You will have to do what works for your family. At our house, anything on a shelf, in its spot in the closet, or in a designated corner of the floor was acceptable. If the boys were in the middle of creating a town or farm with lots of pieces set up, we made a road together through the middle so I could get to the children in the night without destroying the game or myself!

Know that you will have to vary motivators as time passes. A strategy that worked last year might lose its effectiveness this year. Similarly, an approach that didn't work last year might work now, and what one child rejected might appeal to another child.

Forgive the day's offenses before your child goes to sleep. This is mothering motto number three: *Forgive every night!* Clarify as necessary the conflicts of the day and why they happened, and reassure your child of your love and his fresh start the next day.

This is important for you *and* your children. Some nights you will be angry with them for their choices or childish behavior. Other nights you will be angry with yourself for the way you handled a particular situation. If we allow our anger to fester, it will grow into bitterness and resentment, two attributes that don't improve our mothering skills. Find forgiveness for your children *and* yourself before going to sleep, so you can all start fresh the next day.

Pray out loud for your child. Let her hear you thank God for her.

Be firm about having your children stay in their beds. You can tell when they are simply stalling by needing one more glass of water. It's acceptable for you to say "no more," or you can leave the cup of water next to the bed with no refills allowed. If your child is getting out of bed because he is restless or can't sleep, lie down with him for a short time. Some families close the door as a consequence for a child repeatedly crawling out of bed; others give spankings. Whatever the consequence for getting up, it must be immediate. Taking away tomorrow's outing probably won't work (and *you* probably don't want to do that anyway).

Ultimately, staying in bed becomes an issue of obedience to your authority. If they won't obey you when you tell them to stay in bed, they certainly won't obey you later about more important issues. They must stay in bed simply because you are the parent. You are in charge of protecting their best interest, which, in this case, is seeing that they get to bed at a reasonable time.

Be available to *listen* at bedtime. Your children will tell you things in the safety of their beds in the dark that they might not say during the middle of the day. Encourage them to talk to you at this time, even though you are exhausted. You will find they will ask the most amazing questions, and being available to listen will pay long-term dividends when they grow older and you need to hear their hearts on very important matters.

Time Capsule

Naptimes and bedtimes have the potential to be a positive time in both a mother's and a child's day. Give yourself permission to forgive every night. Be committed to the idea that taking naps and getting to bed on time is in your children's best interest. Find naptime and bedtime routines that work for your family. The most immediate benefits are that your children will be less irritable and you will have some predictable time to yourself.

CHAPTER 8

Time for Mom

Now that the kids are napping, or at least in their beds, let's talk about time for Mom. I am into my kids. I love building blanket forts, doing puzzles, and playing soccer in the front yard. But I need time too, to do things for me.

Carol Kuykendall, Director of Communications of MOPS International (Mothers of Preschoolers), often uses the example of mothers frequently feeling like a juice box with ten straws sticking out of it. Each member of your family has stuck a straw in you and is drinking as much of you as they can get. When they are full, you feel as deflated as that poor juice box looks with its sides touching each other. It's

115

no wonder we feel like we have nothing left to give sometimes! We have needs too. But how do we get them met? How do we manage time for us?

You *must* make time for yourself a priority each week, if not every day. In fact, making time for yourself is the basis for mothering motto number four: *Mom time matters!* You may not get as many minutes as you would like and it won't be as often as you prefer, but some time for yourself is better than none.

Start when your children are small to establish that you need some time each day to do *your* stuff. This includes exercising, puttering in your garden, jotting a letter to your sister, or even sitting down to flip through a magazine with your feet up. It's called recharging, and getting even a small chunk of it is valuable, worthwhile time management.

Time to Read

Carry a magazine or book in the car. Every once in a while you will end up waiting—for a doctor, for a preschool class to adjourn, for a friend who is meeting you—and you can get in an article or part of a chapter.

Keep a book handy if you nurse your baby. Depending upon how smoothly the nursing is going, you can sometimes read during that time or after the baby is finished and asleep. Cuddle her and enjoy your book for ten minutes before you put her in her bed. If you are bottle-feeding, you can still enjoy a book and the cuddle time with her after she's finished.

Have "book time" with your kids on the couch before or after lunch. Read two books together, then each of you get your own (they'll need a stack!). Snuggle under an afghan, you on one end and them on the other end with your feet all in the middle, and read for a while. (You may have to do this several times before they get the idea of how this works.) If you want to, you can set a timer and tell them they can't interrupt you until the timer goes off. The length of this reading session will vary by age and attention span. Know that this is not only a break for you, but a valuable gift to your children as you teach them to enjoy books. By giving importance to reading, you are setting a great example for them, and this will help them when they start school.

During your "alone" time, give yourself the gift of reading without undermining your goal for that time. Set a timer for a short period of time, and when the timer goes off, have the discipline to put down the book and get back to your responsibilities without guilt.

TIME TO EXERCISE

The most important element of exercise is finding an activity that you like enough to do on a regular basis! If you hate running, don't buy a baby jogger and plan to run the neighborhood. Consider whether you prefer to exercise at home or at an exercise center, alone or with others. Find something you think you can stick with, then look at your time availability.

At Home

Use an aerobics tape that you can exercise to in the family room. Plan it into your week. If you can't postpone breakfast, then squeeze it in later in the morning, before lunch, after you have played with your children. They can watch, exercise with you, or play on their own.

We all know people who are exercise crazy; find one who can help you plan a series of exercises and stretches for you to do at home. Just fifteen minutes of the right stretches done every day can bring you a long way toward increased strength and muscle tone.

Invest in a treadmill or NordicTrack machine that you power up at home. You can buy these at drastically reduced prices at a used-sports equipment store. The NordicTrack has worked for me after years of nothing else working. Part of the reason I have stuck with it is because I can read while I'm working out. It took a while to get my balance, but it sure makes my workout time seem shorter!

Buy a baby jogger and take your kids for a jog through the neighborhood.

Power walk, pushing your stroller through the neighborhood. Several moms from my MOPS group do this together, and it gives them companionship, conversation, and exercise all at once. If you start, others might see you and join you.

Put a bike seat or bike trailer on your bike and tour the neighborhood with your baby. I loved doing this with my oldest during the short time that I had only one child. He loved it too.

Away from Home

Check out the local fitness center. Many of them have a children's playroom and either provide a baby-sitter during certain hours or allow you to leave your own sitter there supervising your child. If you have a responsible school-age child in your neighborhood, pick her up from school at 3:00 P.M., take her with you to the fitness center, and let her play with your toddler for thirty minutes while you exercise.

Explore the evening hours there too. If your husband works late, evenings can be long for you and the kids. Eat an early dinner, then go to the fitness center. When you return home, you'll be refreshed from your exercise and change of scenery and the kids will be ready to wind down.

Meet your husband at the fitness center. Now you are in the same place at the same time, doing the same thing—amazing! Again, baby-sitting arrangements will vary from family to family, but be creative! Look at different time slots on different days to see if neighbors, family, or friends can trade with you to make this happen.

If you live where it's too cold to exercise outside in the winter, check into area YMCA swimming pools that are open all winter long. Like the fitness center, you will have to work through the child-care possibilities, but it's worth a call to see what the options are for you and your family. Take the kids to meet Dad at the pool after work. Before you leave, you and Dad can take turns swimming some serious laps while the other watches the children or dresses them for the car ride home.

Consider an old hobby that involves exercise. I know several moms who loved horses and rode them quite a bit in their younger years. Now, as mothers of preschoolers, this is their exercise and escape! What is your love? Biking? Volleyball? Horseback riding? Dance? Swimming? Some of these will be harder logistically than others to arrange, but consider what will work for you right now, and go for it.

Walk the malls with your stroller, if you can be disciplined enough not to shop! Most young moms live on tight budgets and sometimes the best way to live within that budget is to stay away from stores. Don't go to the mall if you can't control your spending.

TIME TO THINK

Our world is so hectic that sometimes we need time just to sit. We are designed to function better when we have time without a deadline to reflect on all that is happening around us.

Create a beautiful, comfortable place for yourself in your home to be, as Winnie the Pooh would say, your "Thinking Spot." It might be an overstuffed chair tucked in a corner of a room where no one else goes. It might be the rocker that you use when you feed the baby. It might be the family room couch. It might be the front porch or your apartment's balcony. Claim a place.

Fill a basket with a notepad, pens, perhaps your Bible or a favorite book, maybe even a special snack (that you don't have to share). Take it with you to your thinking spot and curl up with a mug of coffee, hot chocolate, or tea. Listen to the late night or early morning sounds around you. Listen to the birds (or traffic) during the day while the children nap. Give yourself permission for a short time just to *be*. I know your palette is calling, but you will be more effective if you refuel first.

When do you do this? During those brief moments of time when everyone else is occupied. You will have to find a balance between *planning* time for yourself and *discovering* it spontaneously. If you are convinced it is important, you will look for it.

Occasionally splurge on a baby-sitter so that you can have a day or morning or afternoon to yourself. (If your husband works nights or travels quite a bit, take an evening out.) Take this time to do something you can't do with the children along:

- Make a date with another mom for lunch at a *real* restaurant.
- See a matinee movie.
- Go to a bookstore and browse.
- Make an appointment to have your nails done.
- Visit a museum that *you* like.
- Attend a world affairs lecture, theatre production, or symphony concert at a local university.

Time for a Hobby

We moms must selectively choose the hobbies we pursue during this season of our lives. With even minimal time, we can keep up with these hobbies by reading about them and dabbling in them in ways that fit around our family's needs.

If you sew, do needlework, or enjoy crafts, put your name on the mailing list of the local fabric or needlework or craft store. Such stores often offer Saturday afternoon classes on specific subjects or techniques, and someday one of them might work for you as a quick, two-hour getaway.

Gardening is a hobby that has more potential than others during this time because you can turn on the baby monitor and tend to your flowers and plants while the children nap. This hobby is also relatively forgiving when you have to stop midproject!

If you are a mom who paints, think small and portable. Find tools that might fit in your diaper bag so you can really be spontaneous. Take pencils to the park or out to the backyard and draw the children as they play. Sketch the beach you drive by each day on the way out of your neighborhood. Leave ten minutes early for your errands and pull off the road by the wildflowers to capture them with your pastels.

If music is your passion, experiment with different radio stations to surround yourself with the harmonies you love. Find a choir to join (many offer child care during rehearsals). Start playing your instrument again—piano, flute, French horn, guitar. Pull it out and use it as a stress reliever.

If you long to learn more about a subject that interests you, rent an instructional videotape and watch it during naptime or check the local PBS television station for its instructional shows. There's a chance you could arrange your week to watch the one you want to see.

If your husband has weekend responsibilities that conflict with caring for the children, go back to the baby-sitter idea so that you can have time off. We live on a ranch that requires much of my husband's time on the days he is not at his office. When our children were quite small, there was no way he could take care of them *and* handle the ranching chores. If I needed or wanted time away on Saturdays, I often picked up a baby-sitter to be at the house with the babies while Mark attended to the many outside jobs.

We may have to limit our hobbies during the years of small children, but we don't have to give them up altogether. Pick one at a time, and pursue it as best you can.

Be careful that your hobby time doesn't undermine your time with your husband. Sometimes it first appears that the only time you can participate in a hobby is when your husband is available to watch the children. This can be a welcome change of pace for you and valuable time for him with the children. However, there is a danger in regularly pursuing your hobbies instead of spending time with your husband. Be alert to the number of hours you are in activities that pull you away from him. Make those periods of time the exception rather than the rule. Neither husband nor wife likes feeling that he or she must compete with the rest of the world for his or her spouse's time. How can we stay best friends if we never get to be together? Don't let time for your hobby continually have priority over time with your husband.

Time Capsule

During the mothering years we sometimes have to stop and remember that we are women and wives as well as mothers. We need to value those sides of ourselves as much as we value the mothering side and to remember mothering motto number four: Mom time matters! To stay balanced we need time alone, time to read, time to exercise, time to think, and time for a hobby, even if it's only pursued in bits and pieces. For more excellent ideas on moments alone, read *Time Out for Mom . . . Ahhh Moments*, by Cynthia Sumner, another Little Book for Busy Moms.[6]

CHAPTER 9

Remember Your Husband?

CHILDREN CHANGE THE DYNAMIC of a marriage. Now you are not just husband and wife, but also Mom and Dad. We frequently have different expectations of each other as parents than we did as spouses. For example, you might not be bothered by a habit your husband had when he was only your husband, but now that he is also your child's father, you find that you are greatly bothered by that habit. Your husband has not changed from the man he used to be; your expectations of him have changed because he is playing a different role now.

Additionally, most of us parent the way we were parented. Since you and your husband were raised in different families, you may need to clarify why certain parenting routines are important to you. He did not watch *your* dad, so he doesn't know how *you* expect him to act as a father! He will father his children in much the same way as his father cared for him. He also did not watch *your* mom, so he doesn't understand why *you* do certain things. If your mom's style of mothering and his dad's style of fathering aren't blending well, it's time for a heart-to-heart discussion. Your marriage is not in trouble; your different *expectations* of parenting simply need to be adjusted to make your new family work.

FINDING COMMUNICATION

The more deeply we relate to another person, the more we expect that person to "just know" what we think. The fact is, most men do not have that intuition. You need to *tell* your husband what you are thinking. Say what you think, but choose your words carefully—this is the man of your dreams; do not purposely wound him!

Balance unselfishness with the need to communicate your needs and desires. You are partners. Go the extra mile for him, and be sure he knows what would make a difference to you, so he can go the extra mile for you. If you both do more than your share, you both win.

Learn what actions of yours reassure your husband of your love for him. One of Mark's and my favorite books regarding communication in marriage is Gary Chapman's *The Five Love Languages*. According to Chapman, people express love for another person in five primary ways: gift giving, physical touch, acts of service, words of affirmation, and quality time together. His theory is that each of us prefers to be loved in one of these ways more than in the others.[7] Understandably, we use the approach that makes *us* feel loved when we try to communicate love to the people around us. But my husband, and probably yours too, feels most loved by a different approach than I do. Learn what is important to your spouse and approach him from *that* direction.

FINDING MOMENTS

Like everything else in our day, time with our husband will probably come in small segments. When do we find them?

One possibility is early in the morning, before the kids are up. If your husband has a predawn start time at his job, consider getting up with him once a week before daybreak. This would give you some uninterrupted conversation time, if you can be awake enough to think.

Another time that might work is in the evening, after the kids are in bed. Be adamant about the kids' bedtimes, then decide together that you will bring your tasks for the day to a halt at a given time so that you can pay attention to each other. Start on an *easy* night, not one that requires great sacrifice. Consider the day of the week to be sure there's not a conflict, like *Monday Night Football* or another television show you enjoy.

If your children are old enough to enjoy a video, use an occasional video after dinner to entertain them while the two of you talk in another room. This is not cheating; it's practical. I once heard a speaker at a women's retreat say, "Most women don't want to sleep with a man they haven't talked to all day!" Remind him of that.

Another opportunity for spending time with your husband is while your children play. As they grow older, your children will be able to play together with less direct supervision. This will allow you and your husband to talk together nearby.

The minutes following your husband's, and maybe your, arrival home from work might be another good time to spend a few moments together. You'll want to talk with your husband about this sensitive time of day, however, because we all have differing needs. Some parents want to dive into family life as soon as they hit the door; others need solitude to finish unwinding from the day without an onslaught of questions, needs, and requirements dumped on them. Talk about what works for the two of you.

Claim a spot in your home or yard that is for the two of you. Go there together whenever possible. It could be a loveseat, a swing, or a recliner that you pile into together. Mark and I have found comfort in a yard swing that keeps us within earshot of the house through a baby monitor but gives us private time away from the phone and the visual pull of the housekeeping demands.

ROMANCE AT HOME: IN-HOUSE DATES

Although it's fun to get a baby-sitter and go away for the evening, you can also plan at-home dates to claim the time you need together.

Fix a kid-friendly meal early in the evening, and have an adult meal later with just the two of you. Use your better plates and light candles. Ask Dad to handle the baths and bedtime routine while you prepare dinner for the two of you. Or, work together on the kids' baths and bedtime *and* on fixing dinner. This gives you a team approach to finding time together.

Rent a video to watch together. Fix popcorn and Coke floats to add to the ambiance.

Sit in front of the fire together and listen to music. Have a "concert date" with CDs to update him on the music you enjoy. Return the gift by listening to the music he enjoys. Or rent a concert DVD.

Work on the photo albums or some other project together. If you try this you need to communicate the purpose of this time; is it to talk and be together, to conquer the album project, or both? Be clear about your mission, or be frustrated!

Walk around the yard; sit on your porch swing. Use a baby monitor so you can be out there a long time and still have an ear on the kids.

Watch a ball game on television. A pastor's wife I know was speaking to a group of women and said this: "Stop ranting and raving that your husband watches too much television or too many sports. Go sit in his lap and watch it with him!"

Play a game: cards, checkers, chess, backgammon, movie trivia, or Who Wants to Be a Millionaire!

Check out a videotape of dancing lessons, and laugh together as you learn to dance in the privacy of your own home.

Surf the internet together, looking up topics of mutual interest.

Have another couple with a baby come over for the evening. Put the kids to bed and have a potluck dinner and games/conversation with the four adults. Take your playpen to their house next time, and let your baby go to sleep there while you enjoy the evening. Great friendships can be built this way. There is something special about the friends you make and the memories you build with people when your children are small.

Ask your husband to pick up dinner for the two of you on the way home. Adding Chinese take-out or pizza to your evening can give it a lift.

Find an evening when your husband would be willing to barbecue for a change of pace and scenery. Candles work with barbecue too!

Enter each other's hobbies. Learn the lingo and how to recognize the tools or specialties of the subject. Be on the lookout for items of interest in this area. Whether it's sports or woodworking, needlework or antiques, spend time together pursuing that hobby, even if it's not something you get to do often.

Return to the things you loved to do when you dated. If you can't do it, watch a movie about it, revisit a similar site, find a book or museum on the subject, reminisce about those days, and capture the togetherness it brought. Obviously if sailing or water skiing was your love, you can't do those things in a limited time with or without small children. But you could find a lake and take a picnic on a warm weekend, or visit a marina and walk the piers just for the fun of being there again.

DEVELOP TRADITIONS

Look for ways to spice up your marriage with little traditions. Experiment. Something doesn't become a tradition until you've done it more than once, so if you try something and it doesn't work, just discard it and try something else.

- Drink hot chocolate in front of the fire together after the kids go to bed.
- Listen to music together with the lights turned down.
- Watch the news or read the comics together. Watch the entire opening game of each new sports season as the year unfolds.
- Sit on the front porch or apartment balcony together. Look at the lights. Listen to your neighborhood.
- Pick a morning or evening once a week and start praying together for a short time.
- Find something to start doing together twice a month on a regular basis. Put it on the calendar, and pray that the kids don't get sick.

Stick with it for three to six months, then reevaluate.

- Send each other jokes or notes on your e-mail, voice mail, or answering machine. Be silly together. Develop inside jokes that no one else knows.

- Try a teamwork approach to keeping current on world events. One couple I know splits it this way: she reads the daily paper and he reads *Time* magazine. They keep each other informed of the news they're reading and save items of particular interest for the other to look at. This allows them each to stay aware of the world and provokes great conversations. This would be particularly encouraging to a mom who feels like her world is quickly becoming limited to baby information.

- Write a journal back and forth to each other. He can write to you while he's away traveling; you can read it when he returns home and respond for him to read on his next travel assignment.

- Trade favors. Give a back rub or foot rub every night, taking turns. As you serve and receive in turn, your appreciation for each other will grow.

Time Capsule

If there's anything you need time for now that you are a mom, it is time for your marriage.

Protect it.
Build a fortress around it.
Shield and defend it.
Feed it.

Remind your husband that "the best defense is a good offense." Take the offensive together, and make time to *be* together.

CHAPTER 10

Time for God

THE BIRTH OF A CHILD changes our perspective on many issues and ideas, and faith is one of those areas. Many of us are content with our beliefs or lifestyles until a child comes along, and then we think, "Oh, dear, I have to teach them something about God ... but what?!" Until we know what we believe, we cannot teach our children. This becomes our fifth mothering motto: *Pursue God.*

TAKE INVENTORY

Take inventory of your spiritual condition during some of your quiet moments. Review your personal spiritual history. What teachings did you grow up with? Which of them did you embrace? Against which did you rebel? Where did you have questions? Which relationships impacted those ideas?

Consider your perspective today. Now that you are a mother, what different needs and new questions do you have? How do your beliefs impact your daily life and relationships?

Many of the moms I've met through MOPS seek out Christianity when they become mothers. Some are returning to their roots; others want a new perspective on life as they parent. All can find hope and guidance in the teachings of Christ as they take time to learn who he is and what he taught his disciples. How and when do we add pursuing God to the mix of juggling our week's demands?

Do You Have Seven Minutes?

My dear friend and mentor Robert D. Foster wrote a tiny booklet many years ago called *Seven Minutes with God*.[8] In it, he outlines how a regular person like you or me could begin talking to God with just seven minutes of our day. Sometimes that's all a mother has without an interruption! Where can you find seven minutes?

- When you first wake up.
- After your shower.
- In the car after you drop off your child at preschool.

- As you pull into the driveway and discover the kids are both asleep in their car seats.
- At the beginning of naptime.
- During *Blues Clues* or *Sesame Street*.
- While you are walking the dog or out riding your bike or jogging.
- When you are feeding the baby in the night. (Leave your Bible open to the right page wherever you will be sitting. That way, when you stumble in to feed your little one, you can groggily feed your soul as well.)

For most young moms, those seven minutes will be different every day.

Once you find seven minutes, Robert Foster suggests thirty seconds to clear your mind of all the responsibilities and worries calling you, four minutes to read the Bible, and two and a half minutes to pray. Let's look now at what to read and how to pray.

BIBLE READING

Start with the books of Mark or Luke in the Bible. These books contain narrative descriptions of the daily life of Jesus written by men who spent a lot of time with him. Each begins with a short introduction (a sort of "here's my version of what happened"), then launches into the day-to-day encounters each had with all sorts of people. These books are easy to read in short spurts because of their journal type of approach. Daily reading will encourage you as you relive the experiences these men had with Jesus and realize why they came to the startling conclusion that he was the Son of God. Remember, you only have four minutes. Stop at the end of each chapter or when the narrative changes to a new subject. Start at that spot the next day.

Try reading the thirty-one chapters of Proverbs, one each day to correspond with the day of the month. The book of Proverbs is easy to read, full of good advice, and each chapter is independent enough from the previous one that when you miss a day or two, as we all will, you can just pick up on that next day and chapter and keep going.

Purchase a daily devotional that provides both a daily Scripture reading and a few short comments to go along with it. This is an excellent way to learn how a specific verse in the Bible can be relevant to daily life. My current favorite is Max Lucado's *Grace for the Moment*.

Purchase a Bible Study workbook that you can work through alone. These can be topical (Women of the Bible, for example) or can focus on a particular book of the Bible. In four minutes you can read the passage at hand and answer one or two questions. It might take two or three weeks to work through each session, but this is not a race! The process is valuable, the continuity is worthwhile, and the slow pace allows you to absorb the material more deeply than when you are racing through it.

If it has been many, many years since you read the Bible, consider acquiring a new one. Recent printings have updated the biblical language to more modern usage, which is easier to understand. If reading your old Bible feels like reading Shakespeare, consider a new one that will be "regular English" to you.

PRAYER TIME

During your two and a half minutes of prayer time, Robert Foster suggests this outline:

- Acknowledge God for who he is, as Creator and Master of the universe, bigger and more powerful than we can really even comprehend.
- Admit mistakes, failings, fears, goof-ups, bad judgments, lost tempers, etc.
- Thank God for loving us anyway, for sending Jesus to be our Savior, for rescuing us from specific problems, for providing specific gifts, blessings in our lives, for answering specific prayers and concerns of the week.

- Tell God what our concerns are today and ask
  for his help in specific areas, with specific relationships, and with specific worries. (This is a
  good time to ask God to answer specific questions you may have about your faith or spiritual issues.)

Soon you will find that you desire more than
seven minutes with God each day. When this happens, separate the Bible reading time from the
prayer time. Read in the morning for seven minutes
and pray in the afternoon for seven minutes. If your
afternoon time gets booby-trapped, pray the next
morning. If you make time to do this, God will
return to you the minutes you spend. He can alter
your circumstances, change the demands on your
time, and clarify your priorities so that you have time
for this *and* for the other important parts of your day.
I have seen him do it in my life and in lives around
me for twenty-five years.

OTHER MOMENTS WITH GOD

Remember "arrow prayers." As author Hope
McDonald says, arrow prayers are "the kind of
prayers we shoot up to God all day long. It is the
natural turning to God throughout the day—sharing with Him our feelings, our happiness, our hurts
and disappointments."[9] My most often uttered arrow

prayer is "Lord, there's too much to do! Show me what is important; show me again my priorities. Show me which task to do first. Please take some of these other things away and give me the contentment to live with all that is left undone!"

Memorize Bible verses. Write a meaningful verse on a notecard and stick it on the mirror to look at while you brush your teeth or apply your mascara. Put one on the windowsill over your kitchen sink or on the refrigerator door. Author Cynthia Heald says this was a significant positive influence in her life when her four children were small and it was impossible to get out of the house for Bible study.[10] Learn a new verse each week or every two weeks.

If you can, find another mom to be a partner with you as you memorize. This will be more fun than doing it alone, and will help you both stay on track better.

Find a women's Bible study. MOPS is not a Bible study, but many churches that host MOPS also offer a midweek Bible study, often with child care provided.

Find a couple's Bible study offered during Sunday school or during an evening. This time spent with your husband discussing material you've both read is beneficial to both of you. The added companionship of other couples will encourage you as well.

Fill your home with music that reminds you of the Lord. Whatever style you like, fill your head with lyrics that praise him and remind you of his faithfulness.

Keep a blessing jar. My friend Terry, mother of two, did this one year. As the weeks unfolded, she and her children wrote down the blessings they saw from God each day. These little papers went into a jar on the counter. When one of them was discouraged, Terry pulled out a handful of papers to remind them of God's faithfulness to them in days past. These papers became tangible offers of hope for God's faithfulness in the days ahead.

Find a prayer partner. Pray for her each day and give her specific concerns of yours that she can pray for you.

GET INVOLVED IN CHURCH

Attending church services when your children are very young is a challenge. Between the truckload of supplies you must take with you, concerns about contagious diseases in the nursery, and overall fatigue, it sometimes just doesn't seem worth it! Be patient with yourself and consider the following suggestions.

Find a church close to home. You will be more likely to get to church if it's nearby, and it will be easier for you to have a sense of community with the other people there when you happen to meet them at the grocery store or the local park.

Give yourself permission to start slowly. Go every other week or every third week as you start getting used to venturing out with a baby.

If the kids are sick often or it's too hard to get the entire family ready, alternate with your husband, one of you staying home and one of you going to church.

Look again at your overall weekly activities and priorities discussed in Chapter 1 to see if church is bumping into another priority. What can you do to keep them from colliding? Give yourself time to sort it out. Don't give up.

Check out the child-care setup at the church. Find out what precautions are taken to keep your child well, so that you can be comfortable leaving him there in the nursery. What is the policy on taking babies into the worship service? It is hard to focus on the worship or teaching when little wigglers are next to you, but having the baby there with you for a few weeks or months may be a better solution than not going at all.

Do what you can to rethink Saturday nights so that getting up for church the next morning is less painful. Ending the evening earlier on Saturday will make Sunday more enjoyable.

Use the getting-out-the-door strategies in Chapter 4 to help make Sunday morning go more smoothly.

Have an easy breakfast ready for Sunday mornings.

If you or your husband work late on Saturdays or have a Sunday morning shift, look for a Sunday night worship time. Many churches have them.

TEACH YOUR CHILDREN

The Bible says, "These commandments that I give you today are to be upon your hearts. Impress them on your children. Talk about them when you sit at home and when you walk along the road, when you lie down and when you get up" (Deuteronomy 6:6–7).

Teaching our children about faith is a daily thing in the midst of life. Talk to them about your faith, about the answers to your prayers, about the ways in which you see God active in your life. When you talk about God, you give your children a sense of God's presence, even though they can't see him. Many of us talk to our children about our trusted friends or about our parents who live far away, because we want them to know about these people even though they do not live near us. We can give our children that same sense of awareness of God by talking about him.

Find a children's Bible or devotional book to read at breakfast or bedtime. There are many, many children's Bible storybooks, stories about Jesus, activity books about Jesus, coloring books with Bible stories, and so on, starting with the most simple words, illustrations, and summaries. We have found bedtime to be less rushed than breakfast for these stories. As they grow, your children will absorb more and more of the lesson. Learning the story is just the first part; later they will understand the depth of its meaning and the layers of truth to be found within it.

Use music. Kids love hearing other kids sing, and there are lots of kids' songs available on tape and CD that teach Bible verses and principles with an upbeat melody. The message of a song becomes another teaching opportunity as you say to them, "Do you know what that song means?" One of our favorite series is the Hide 'em in Your Heart series by Steve Green, which puts specific verses to music. It is a wonderful way for children to memorize Scripture.

Use life to teach. As you drive by an ambulance pray aloud for the people in it. As you pass the wildflowers, point out God's creation. When the evening news reveals horrible things, pray with your children that God will send help to those in need.

Find simple Bible verses for the whole family to learn. Other moms, your child's Sunday school teacher, MOPPETS teacher, or preschool teacher might have some easy ones to suggest as a starting point. There are a number of very short verses in the Bible that are meaningful, or you can have the youngest children learn only the first part of a verse for starters:

Proverbs 3:5	"Trust in the LORD." (Later: "Trust in the LORD with all your heart.")
1 John 4:14	"The Father has sent the Son . . ." (Later: "The Father has sent the Son to be the Savior of the world.")
Ephesians 4:28	"Let him who steals, steal no longer."
Ephesians 4:25	"Speak truth, each one of you."
Acts 16:31	"Believe in the Lord Jesus Christ and you shall be saved."
1 Corinthians 13:4	"Love is patient, love is kind."

Alternate those which are highly practical (love is patient) with those that teach more abstract truth (the Father has sent the Son) so that your children learn the Bible holds both types of wisdom.

Explore video series that agree with your perspective on life. Veggie Tales videos meet kids on their own level with stories that are Bible-based but retold through a new story on a child's level. There are many others to choose from. Use all television and video time to reinforce ideas you want your children to learn. This doesn't mean showing exclusively Bible-based videos, but it does mean being aware of the input your kids are getting through video and asking yourself *each time* if this is the content you want your kids to absorb.

Take advantage of the preschool years to plant seeds of faith that can grow without the tangles of peer pressure, social pressure, and confusing questions. As an adult, you know that life sometimes presents difficult questions and that the journey of faith isn't always simple and easy. Your children haven't bumped into those difficulties yet. Use the preschool years to teach them that God is trustworthy, so they will be able to stand on that foundation when the hard questions come. See the book *Opening Your Child's Spiritual Windows* by Cheri Fuller[11] for more ideas along this vein.

Pray aloud with your children at bedtime. Let your child hear you thank God for him and for the privilege you have of being his mom. Let them hear you ask God, "Help me be a good mom to these girls. Help me to understand them well."

Time Capsule

The search for spiritual answers is a lifelong journey that strongly impacts the way we approach mothering, the value we place on our children's lives, and the principles upon which we raise them. This leads to our fifth mothering motto: Pursue God. Take time to deepen your understanding of your faith by reading the Bible and praying. Then teach your children what you have learned. You are the most influential person in your child's life. Use that position to plant and grow seeds of faith in their lives. Nothing is a better use of your time.

CHAPTER 11

Finding Flexibility

WHEN WE TOOK OUR two sons, then ages three years and four and a half years, to the circus one summer, I was struck by the parallels I discovered between the "Greatest Show on Earth" and my daily routine. Our seats high above the floor offered a great overview of the show, but even then it was impossible to watch everything at once. I thought, *This is how I feel every day—three things going on at one time with none of them capturing my full attention!*

Doesn't the circus remind you of mothering? Sometimes we are lion tamers; other times we walk the tightrope of diplomacy with family, friends, neighbors, and children. We are always juggling needs, wants, priorities, relationships, finances, and responsibilities. And even when we are weary, the show must go on!

My prayer is that this book has given you new hope as you juggle the pieces of your life. Little ones require a whole new flexibility on our part if we are going to experience the joy of mothering. Don't miss the joys! There will *always* be more to do than we can do well. Let go of the pieces that are stressing you out so that you can enter your children's world and experience life with them—because you can't replay those moments. *You* will benefit more. *You* will find more joy in your mothering. Put down the adult parts of your day for a while, then be flexible with the remaining pieces when you return to them.

Being flexible means finding a balance between commitment to plans we've already made and adaptability to the spontaneous changes that occur with a moment's notice. If we are not committed to the priorities we have established, we will be tossed about like the wind and never accomplish anything. On the other hand, there are always new possibilities waiting for us, and there often will be valid reasons to change direction in order to better care for our families. Being flexible means accepting that our days will be a continual tug-of-war between these two positions, without being angry about it. Ah . . . there's the rub!

Why do we get angry? My pastor says we get angry when someone has blocked our progress toward a goal or desire. That happens a lot in a mother's day. Sometimes we think we alone are the only ones having to stop, start, stop, start all day long. Be encouraged. The rest of us moms are doing that too. It's only human to be disappointed when we have looked forward to certain plans and they fall through. Accept disappointment at its face value, cry if you need to, then find a way to go on. Staying angry won't make you feel better.

Motherhood is not a predictable stage of life. Finding flexibility means knowing how to accommodate changing plans and knowing when to stick with the original plan. Only then can we make the most of the unexpected moments that really matter. Ironically, being flexible in one situation gives us greater freedom to stick with our original plan another time when it is the better choice.

Learning to be flexible will also keep your family moving forward and reduce your feelings of failure. You can't schedule or plan around colicky nights, refusals to actually sleep at naptime, or a shoelace that breaks as you head out the door. Having the flexibility to navigate around and through these situations as they pop up will leave you with a better attitude about what you *have* managed to accomplish.

In review, take a hard look at your priorities. Know in the midst of your day that your time is valuable and that you are spending it in accordance with an overall concept of what is important to *your* family.

Figure out a way to plan your week and keep track of your responsibilities in a format that works for you and allows you to roll with the unexpected twists and turns it will take.

Try thinking in pieces and tackling your activities in smaller segments. Work as a team; find helpful chores your children can do. Remember, progress counts! Bring a little more order to your home, at least in places that make a difference.

Spend time with your children first. Make sure they know they are important to you. Play every day! Let them help you with the household needs. Then teach them the value of time playing alone and together while you tackle the responsibilities you have that they cannot help you do. Remember the value of the intangibles in your week: togetherness, patience, discovery, trust. These are important! They take time.

Find time to nurture yourself, to pursue your interests: Mom time matters.

Be committed to naptimes and pleasant bedtimes. Forgive every night.

Spend time with your husband. Invest in him. Believe in him.

Pursue God. Have the courage to seek out the truth about him. Know what you believe and why, and teach it to your children.

Find flexibility. Parenting is full of detours. Expect the unexpected and move ahead anyway.

Enjoy your children. Each is a gift from God with unique personalities, strengths, and struggles. Rejoice in them. When it's all said and done, this season is only for a short time. Our adult years are counted in five or six decades; the years of small children will number only a fraction of those. Yet the time management gains you achieve now can impact your family for the rest of your children's growing-up years. As long as we are mothers, we will have too much to do. Equip yourself with the confidence that you can handle it; for you know how to juggle.

Notes

1. Elisa Morgan and Carol Kuykendall, *What Every Child Needs* (Grand Rapids: Zondervan, 1997), 74.

2. Leigh Rollar Mintz, *Kids' Stuff and What to Do with It* (Grand Rapids: Zondervan, 2000).

3. Ross Campbell, M.D., *How to Really Love Your Child* (Wheaton, Ill.: Victor Books, 1985), 32–36.

4. Ibid.

5. Florence Littauer, *Raising the Curtain on Raising Children* (Dallas: Word Publishing, 1988), 185–95.

6. Cynthia Sumner, *Time Out for Mom . . . Ahhh Moments* (Grand Rapids: Zondervan, 2000).

7. Gary Chapman, *The Five Love Languages* (Chicago: Northfield Publishing, 1992).

8. Bob Foster, *Seven Minutes with God* (Colorado Springs: Challenge Books, 1960).

9. Hope McDonald, *Discovering How to Pray* (Grand Rapids: Zondervan, 1976), 19.

10. Cynthia Heald, presentation to Northeast Bible Church, San Antonio, Texas, February 8, 2001.

11. Cheri Fuller, *Opening Your Child's Spiritual Windows* (Grand Rapids: Zondervan, 2001).